JOURNEY THROUGH MANY MANSIONS

Navigating Grief and Understanding Mediumship

DANIEL JOHN

Library of Congress Control Number: 2022911913

ISBN 13: 979-8-218-08847-7

10 9 8 7 6 5 4 3 2 1

"In my Father's house are many mansions: if *it were* not *so*, I would have told you. I go to prepare a place for you."
(John 14:2) (KJV)

Think about it, there must be higher love
Down in the heart or hidden in the stars above
Without it, life is wasted time
Look inside your heart, I'll look inside mine

Lyrics from the song, "Higher Love," written by Steve Winwood and Will Jennings. Produced by Steve Winwood and Russ Titelman.

Alex, Sammy, Stella, Johnny, and Mom:

Thank you for being my true motivation in making this world a better place. Thank you for the support and love each of you provide me every single day! I promise to do this work with the sole intent to provide love to all those who are put in my path. I will continue to give each of you every single ounce of love and energy I can in order to be the best husband, father, and son you could ever ask for. I love you all!

CONTENTS

INTRODUCTION

We have all experienced defining moments in our lives which we will never forget. Personally, for me, one of the most significantly defining moments was when my father died. I will never forget the phone call I received when Dad passed away. It took years to navigate through the physical loss of my father and understand the grief I felt from that experience.

I am writing this book to help you navigate through your own grief, specifically as it relates to the passing of a loved one. I want to tell you that you are not alone. It is completely normal to go through a process we call grief, with the ultimate goal of getting to an acceptance stage of the loss you've experienced. This book is intended to help you with that.

I have been a practicing medium for about four years now. Before you put the book down or get scared about that word, please let me help you understand what I do. To put it simply, I am a channel or conduit for God/Spirit, as are you. I will explain this further as you continue reading, but for now, just understand that I teach eternal life. From all my experience, I firmly believe that we do not die. Our soul continues on an infinite journey through many realms, realities, and experiences (mansions). Forever.

I understand that life after death is a hard concept for some of you to believe, but please stick with me. For other readers, you may have had experiences that all but prove there is some sort of reality or consciousness after we die. Wherever you fall in that spectrum, please know that you picked up this book for a very specific reason. Take the time to enjoy the information I will share with you in the pages that follow, so you can better navigate through life after experiencing the physical loss of someone you truly love and miss.

As a medium, I am able to connect with the souls of people who have passed away from this realm but continue to live in another reality or "mansion." "Spirit," as I call it, has a plethora of information that can be extremely helpful to us here in the physical world. In my first book, "Why Are We Here? Reflections on Life from a Spiritual Medium," I wrote about how I came to understand my gift as a medium and what I've learned about life since being able to communicate with the spirit world. In the later chapters of that book, I briefly mentioned how mediumship works, while also sharing some experiences from some of my mediumship sessions. In this book, I have decided to give you a more in-depth look at how mediumship works, why most mediums do this work, and how a session with a medium can drastically improve your life by helping you better navigate through your grief.

If you read my first book, you will notice a few repeating themes in this one. I am writing this book assuming you have not read, "Why Are We Here?" If you have read it, the minimal amount of repeating information will be a good refresher for you.

I feel if more people recognized and appreciated communication with the spirit realms, the world would be a significantly more peaceful place to live. Spirit communication can often be a difficult concept to grasp, but by the time you put this book down after reading it completely, I feel very confident you will have a much better understanding of what mediumship/spirit communication is, how it works – for me at least – and why it is so beneficial to us as human beings, especially to those who are grieving.

If you have an open mind, an open heart, and you are willing to accept that there are things in this world and universe that are beyond our limited understanding and language, you will be better equipped to experience life in an exponentially more meaningful and powerful way. All too often, we, as human beings, let our experiences and beliefs form our reality with an extremely limited perspective. All I ask of you is that as you read this book, you put everything you think you know on hold for the time being.

Please accept that you do not know everything, and the beliefs you currently have may very well change after reading this book. Beliefs are not truths; they are what you *believe* to be true. My beliefs have changed drastically over the past few years, and they continue to change every single day. I remember having a conversation with a former coworker a few years ago, and he said to me, "My beliefs will never change." At the time, I thought that was very admirable, but if you think about it, if you are not willing to change your beliefs, that can only mean you think you know everything, and you don't.

There is a significant amount of content in this book that may seem hard to believe and may even appear illogical at times. As you read, please know my intention is for you to experience nothing but love as you begin to understand how we, as human beings, can connect with the "spirit world," which is what I believe to be our true "Home."

Over the past four years in which I have communicated with the spirit world, I have had experiences that are nothing short of unexplained miracles. I will share many of these stories with you in this book. Mediumship is something I believe every single one of us can experience. I will say this over and over, but you do not need someone who says they are a "medium" in order to connect with God/Spirit, or your loved ones who have passed away. I am sure many of you have had spiritual experiences that cannot be explained. We will cover many of these phenomena in this book as well.

I have provided well over 2,500 mediumship/guidance sessions, many to those who are severely grieving the loss of a loved one. I have read hundreds of books about near-death experiences (NDEs), death and dying, life after death, theology, religion, spirituality, and mediumship. I have taken mediumship development and astrology classes. I have also been studying the Bible for many years. I am a Reiki master and certified medium. I have a lot to share with you, so get ready to experience the unconditional love that God/Spirit has for you, and for every single one of us.

I will use the words, "God," "The Universe," "Holy Spirit," "Sprit," "Source," "It," "The Other Side," "Love," and "Spirit World," interchangeably throughout this book. In my opinion, they are all words we use to describe something that is beyond words and surpasses our limited understanding. When I use, "He," "She," "It," or any other pronoun to describe this "Thing," I will also use those interchangeably as well.

Thank you for taking the time to read the pages that follow. I promise I will do my best to leave you better off in life and even more full of love than before you picked up this book.

—Daniel John

CHAPTER 1

NAVIGATING THE LOSS OF A LOVED ONE

Your loved one has passed away. The services are over, and the family and friends have stopped visiting. The calls and texts have slowly come to an end, and you are not receiving any more sympathy cards in the mail. *Now, what?* Everyone has returned to their "normal life," but you are having a difficult time doing so. You miss the person, or people, who have passed away and *you* can't get back to your "normal life." You are sad, you are stuck, and you don't have the energy to get through this. *Let me help you.*

First of all, I am sorry for your loss. I understand that you picked up this book with the intention of receiving some guidance, so I will not let you down. There is hope. There is relief. There is a light at the end of the tunnel. You are going to be okay. Your loved one is okay. In fact, from what I understand, our loved ones who have passed away are more than okay. Believe it or not, they are better than we are here on Earth. Way better.

As a medium, part of my job is to teach eternal life and love, connect people here in the physical world with the energy of their loved ones, and let God/The Universe use me as a conduit to spread His/Its' unconditional eternal love. Please believe me when I tell you that when we die, even though we leave our physical body, the true part of us, the soul, does not die. Our souls are eternal. That means that your loved ones still exist, they are still with you, and their energy and love never dies. Ever.

Yes, you miss your loved one's physical presence, but please know they are literally still with you. They know what is going on in your life, they know about new babies and life events, and most importantly, they know and can experience the love, thoughts, and prayers that you continue to provide to them every day throughout your physical journey here on Earth. Our loved ones who have passed away before us are more alive than we can imagine, and we can affect them in a significantly positive way with a simple prayer/positive thought to them in spirit. I don't mean to sound cliché and say that "your loved ones are always with you," but seriously, they are. They are with you more than you can comprehend.

Knowing that your loved ones who have passed away are still with you is the first step to healing. This is not a "feel-good" fabrication I am making up to help you feel better. This is what I firmly believe to be true, and it is what has been communicated to me by spirit for many years. Think of it this way: You are energy, and energy cannot be created or destroyed; it just changes form. So, your loved ones still exist, they are just experiencing a different reality than you are. But I believe those who have passed away can also view, experience, and influence *this* reality as well. *Make sense?*

When you truly believe in eternal life, it can take a significant burden off the heart. According to what spirit has shared with me over the years, not only do our loved ones in spirit still exist, they are also experiencing a blissful state that the Earth plane cannot provide. Therefore, it would be in your best interest to be happy for them. However, you are still on this Earth for a very specific reason.

Understanding that your loved one is "there," and you are "here," is one of the main steps to healing. You are important to God's plan right where you are. You are needed on this Earth to complete a very specific mission that has yet to be completed, which is why you are still "here." Trust that. Believe that, and honor God's plan even if you don't like it.

Now that you can start to understand and believe that your passed loved ones are still alive, they are still with you energetically, and they are in a state of bliss in the spirit world, there is still the loss of their physical presence you must deal with. You miss their touch or verbal conversation, and that can be difficult to accept. Even though I am going to explain mediumship in this book, you can feel, sense, and "know," that your loved ones in spirit can communicate with you without a "medium." I will illustrate that our loved ones in spirit are constantly reaching out to us, continually guiding us, and they are always providing love to us from "the other side." We just need to adjust our dial/antenna to be open to receiving this love. Being able to connect with your loved ones in spirit, can be, and most often is, more healing than what years of traditional therapy can provide.

Before you go running to a medium for guidance or support, please take some time to pray and read through this book, as it will help you better understand how communication with the spirit world works. This explanation of mediumship will allow you to be better prepared, when and if, you feel inspired to visit a medium yourself, or when you decide you are ready to connect with your loved ones in spirit on your own without a medium, which is the end goal. You will hear me say just a few times throughout this book that you don't need to consult a "medium" or "psychic" to be able to connect to the spirit world. God/Spirit/The Holy Spirit/your loved ones are available to you at all times. You just need to know the best way to connect with spirit.

Eventually, over time, you will heal, and you will be okay. Soon, you will be able to participate in your life with just as much, if not more, energy and love than before your loved one passed away. Please trust the grief process. You will get to the point where you can accept the physical loss of your loved one. You may never like it, but you will come to accept that your loved one's passing is part of your reality and it's also part of a well-organized Divine plan. You will fulfill your very meaningful and specific purpose for your life here on Earth. Connecting with God/Spirit, along with the energies of your loved ones who have passed, will guide you to downright bliss and abundance.

CHAPTER 2

WHAT THE HECK IS A "MEDIUM" AND HOW IN THE WORLD DOES "MEDIUMSHIP" WORK?

The word "medium" means "middle," so a medium is someone who receives information from the spirit world and then communicates that information to a person who is physically here on Earth. Whether you believe in mediums or not, I urge you to read this chapter with an open mind. A few years ago, I never would have believed that not only am I a medium, but that I would write multiple books about grief and mediumship.

If you asked me five years ago if it were possible to communicate with "the dead," I probably would have said that ability is not a real thing. I had heard of people communicating with people/souls who have passed away, but I honestly never gave it much thought. Not only did I not believe that we could communicate with people who have passed away, I thought that when we die, we went to "Heaven" or "hell" and that was it. Boy, was I wrong about that. As a point of information for you, the reader, please note that I have chosen not to capitalize "hell," because it is my opinion that "hell" is not a place. I also will not capitalize "satan," or "the devil," because I feel they do not exist outside of human perception and ego.

I'm a major skeptic by nature, and it took a long time, an extremely open mind, many books, and many mediumship sessions, to actually believe that spirit communication is not only possible, but also that it is extremely beneficial, especially to those who are grieving the loss of a loved one. It wasn't until one night out in Boston in early 2017, that I started to change my mind about what happens to us when we "die."

As a medical sales representative for over eighteen years, I have been to many cities around the country for sales meetings and work events. I am currently with my third company in that span, but the first thirteen years were spent with a company whose corporate office was located in Boston, Massachusetts. While at one such meeting, at least two lives would change forever.

Often, after our daily sales meetings, our company would take the sales team out to dinner. I really enjoyed these dinners because they were usually at restaurants I otherwise would not have gotten the chance to experience. At dinner one evening after our work meeting, I sat next to a woman named Deirdre, whom I had just met for the first time earlier that day. Deirdre is a very nice middle-aged woman who did mention she was a recent widow when she introduced herself to the team as a new sales rep earlier that day. I thought nothing of this as I sat next to her to enjoy dinner at one of the best Italian restaurants in downtown Boston.

While eating our appetizers, I was suddenly overcome with a flood of information. Throughout my life, there have been many times when I have been guided to give someone certain information that ended up being extremely helpful to the receiver. That being said, these types of situations didn't happen often, and I never gave it much thought because helping others is my absolute favorite thing to do. However, this time it was different. I was inundated with an abundance of information that was hard to understand, and it was extremely difficult to communicate what I was feeling. It all felt kind of weird, to be honest.

I still don't know how I obtained the information I was receiving, but I did. I wasn't thinking about Deirdre's deceased husband, and I completely forgot that she told us earlier that day about being recently widowed. I fought "the feelings" at first, but they continued to get stronger and stronger, so I finally spoke up.

For a good forty-five minutes, others at the table were wondering what was going on as Deirdre and I laughed, then cried, and then laughed again, over and over. I didn't know why, and I sure didn't know how, but we realized that the energy of Deirdre's deceased husband, Bob, was communicating with us from the spirit world. Wherever he was, Bob was able to pass on very specific, validating, and most of all, loving and helpful messages to his wife. From names of family members to specific detailed information about their children – who I obviously knew nothing about – to nicknames and inside jokes, to private current events, to extremely intimate special moments, this "reunion" was absolutely beautiful. To this day, even after performing thousands of mediumship sessions since then, that night in Boston was one of the most amazing experiences I have ever had.

After an abundance of healing, much laughter, and many tears, dinner was brought to the table. We thought Bob was done communicating at that point, but we were wrong. As we were both sitting there in awe, eating our delicious meals (I remember I had Chicken Parmesan), one word kept playing over and over in my head: "Butterfly."

Butterfly. . . just say, butterfly. Butterfly!

Just as before, I tried to fight the feeling, but it kept getting stronger and stronger. Finally, as I could not take it anymore, I grabbed the parmesan cheese shaker and uncomfortably slammed it on the table and said, "Butterfly! I have to say 'butterfly,' and I almost feel like there is something funny about it."

Deirdre immediately started to cry and then laugh almost uncontrollably. What she did next, completely shocked me. She pulled down the back of her shirt to show the butterfly tattoo on her shoulder that included the names of her children displayed in the wings!

My immediate skeptic response to her was, "Were you wearing a shirt earlier today where I could have seen that?"

She responded with a snarky, but loving, "I am wearing the same shirt I've had on all day." The shirt completely covered the entire tattoo. Needless to say, we were both in awe.

"What about the humor?" I asked. "I can almost hear him laughing." I felt uncomfortable that Bob was communicating a feeling of humor while Deirdre was quite visibly emotional.

Deirdre said, "There was an ongoing joke in which he said he would never get the same tattoo, even though the whole family wanted him to get it."

Wow!

I will never forget the hug Deirdre gave me after that dinner. It was so full of love and appreciation. She said words to me in that moment that I will forever cherish.

"I have been waiting for this! Thank you so much!" she said.

I didn't know this at the time, but Bob passed away suddenly and instantly. They never got a chance to say goodbye to each other. Bob and Deirdre were married for over thirty years, and he was "gone" without any warning. The moments we shared at dinner allowed Deirdre to get the closure she needed, and the connection enabled her to experience the eternal love her husband still has for her even though he was not there physically. What an experience!

As you might imagine, I could barely sleep that night. I had so many questions. I probably had some of the same ones you may be thinking at this very moment. *What just happened? How did that all work? Where was Bob when he was 'communicating' with me? Why couldn't I see him with my eyes or hear him with my ears? How did that information come to me? Was it really her husband, Bob, communicating with me, or were they just lucky guesses on my part? Did I just make all that stuff up?*

But the information was so accurate and very specific.

Did I read her mind? Because that would not be cool. But I couldn't have. Why was some of the information not confirmed while most of it was? Why me? Should I do this for other people because it obviously helped her? I love helping others. Should I tell anyone? How would I even begin to tell anyone what just happened?

That was the beginning of my ongoing mediumship journey in which I continue to learn from and grow through every single day. As you continue reading this book, I will do my best to answer many of the aforementioned questions. I will try to help you understand what I experienced that night and share with you some of the magical moments I have witnessed in the five years since.

JOURNEY THROUGH MANY MANSIONS

Mediumship is hard for most people to believe. It's hard to understand and it's just plain "weird," in my opinion. Through mediumship however, I have been able to experience firsthand, some of the most wonderful reunions, amazing healings, miraculous personal transformations, and pure unconditional love that a human being can experience. Whether I am in a session with a client, or I receive information for someone while I'm in public – which doesn't happen too often – mediumship works the same way when I feel a spirit wanting to connect with a loved one here on Earth.

The simplest way I can describe how communication with the spirit world works, is that it is like a game of charades. Spirit will communicate by simply impressing thoughts in my mind. It kind of feels like I am making things up, but over time, I have pragmatically concluded that extremely valuable, detailed, and specific information often comes directly from the spirit world. Spirit will impress information in my mind, such as numbers, names, symbols, analogies, songs, animals, Bible verses, pictures, smells, feelings, and so much more. I must figure out what the spirit is trying to communicate, and then pass those messages on to whomever the messages are intended. In my opinion, the sole purpose of spirit communication is love. There is no other reason. It's simply love.

Besides numbers and names, one of the most common ways spirit communicates, at least with me, is by showing me one of my symbols. These symbols have been developed over the years during the thousands of mediumship sessions spirit has delivered through me. I, along with the help of spirit, have built what most mediums call a "spirit dictionary." This is simply a list of symbols that can mean one, or a few very specific things for me during a mediumship session. I will give you a few examples so you can grasp the idea.

Before I explain some of my symbols, it's important to understand that I don't see or hear spirit. The best way I can describe my communication with spirit is that I feel and sense information from them. So, when I say that I "see" something, or I say they "show me" something, remember, it is simply a thought that enters my mind.

For instance, when spirit "shows me" Twinkies®, it means I must talk about twins, but sometimes it means that I must mention the actual tasty treat. Once during a session, I received the thought of "Twinkies®" while channeling a woman's deceased mother. As I shared what I was receiving with my client, when she couldn't validate the siblings or the snack, she explained that she and her mother were Minnesota Twins season ticket holders. They went to many games together and this was her mother's way of sharing how much she loved attending them with her.

When I "see" the action figure GI Joe®, it means I must mention someone in the military. There have been multiple times when the person I am meeting with not only has a close friend or family member who is/was in the military, that person is actually named "Joe" as well. When I "think of" glitter, or pixie dust, it is my symbol for confirming that the spirit was with the sitter (the person receiving messages in a mediumship session is often referred to as "the sitter"), or someone known by the sitter, while they were sick or injured here in the physical world. When I "feel" a straight blade razor, it is the spirit's way to inform me that they were solely responsible for their own passing. When I "sense" pickles, I must either talk about a new baby or actual pickles. I have had symbols mean four or five different things with just one single impression. Here is an example:

I was in a group mediumship session speaking with a woman whose father was "coming through" strongly. I explained to her that I was receiving an intense feeling to mention raisins. I further explained that raisins are my symbol for California, but it can also mean physical raisins. I told her there was a feeling of love behind the raisins, so I wasn't sure whether it was the state of California or the fruit.

The woman immediately began to cry. What she said next is just one small example of how awesome spirit can be:

"My father passed away a few months ago. He lived in California," she said. "While we were out west," she continued, "I had to clean out his car and that was very tough for me. While I was cleaning out his trunk, I found four California Raisins figurines in it. They were the solar ones, the kind you put on your dashboard, so the sun charges them, and they dance. So, as I was crying and missing Dad, I placed them on the car, and they all started dancing. I felt him at that exact moment," she said.

That is just one of thousands of awesome experiences I have had over the past few years. Whether I "hear" a song, "sense" a personality, "feel" a symbol, or "taste" or "smell" something, please understand that I am not using any of my five senses. It is a sixth sense that doesn't register in the same way as how you would experience something in your daily life. It is different, and it takes time to recognize and interpret what is being sent to me by spirit.

We all have the ability to communicate with the spirit world. How can you become better at picking up subtle hints from your loved ones in spirit? Meditate, pray, exercise, eat properly, and most of all, love. What do I mean by "love?" Treat others how you want to be treated. (Matthew 22:39) and (1 Peter 4:8-9). Practice the Golden Rule. Don't judge. Forgive. Be a good ethical person and walk the walk. It is that simple.

The more you take the path of love and listen to what the true essence of you is trying to tell you, the more you can tune into your soul, which in my opinion, is who you actually are. Love. "Love" is the best word to describe who we are as souls. My first book, "Why Are We Here? Reflections on Life from a Spiritual Medium," is all about how you can be your best self. So, if you have not read it, it may be a good idea to pick it up. I am sure you will enjoy it.

Please know that you can't understand mediumship and how it works in one small book and much less by reading one short chapter. What I can tell you is that this intimate explanation of mediumship and how it works, will allow your mind to think a little outside the box, and at the same time create a desire to learn a little more about how mediumship/two-way spirit communication works. When you can truly believe that your loved ones who have passed away are very much alive, this will in turn help you heal. They are just in another room or mansion.

CHAPTER 3

MISCONCEPTIONS ABOUT MEDIUMSHIP

To help you better understand what mediums do, it is important to clear up many of the common misconceptions about mediums and mediumship. Mediumship – two-way communication with the spirit world – has existed and has been continuously documented for thousands of years. Since that is the case, many untrue stories, theories, frauds, and many other misunderstandings have surfaced. Let's address many of these misconceptions right off the bat:

Are there fake mediums (charlatans) out there? Absolutely. *Are there mediums who are giving mediumship sessions with not the best of intentions?* Unfortunately, I believe so. In this chapter I will clear up some common misunderstandings about mediumship, illustrate what a genuine medium does, and explain why most of us do this work.

Being able to connect with passed loved ones in spirit with the intention of helping the grieving here on Earth is a beautiful gift. Everyone has the ability to communicate with spirit, but each of us are blessed with certain specific gifts that we can use to help others. (1 Peter 4:10) and (1 Corinthians 12:4-7). For me, and for many other mediums, our purpose is to help people heal from the grief that can often result from the physical loss of a loved one, and to teach eternal life (God). In my opinion, being a medium is a job and a gift at the same time. Please also remember that this gift/ability is something that is quite challenging and time consuming. There is a significant amount of personal sacrifice that a medium must commit to, in order to serve others and to serve God. (Luke 12:48). In my opinion, those who are practicing mediumship for all the right reasons (love), are using their God-given gifts to serve others.

One of the things that concerned me after my experience with Deirdre, was the possibility that I had read her mind. *What if the information I was getting wasn't from her late husband, Bob, but it was just information that she was giving me subliminally without either of us knowing?*

Here is why I firmly believe that when I have a session with a client, the information is absolutely coming from the spirit realm. In approximately 90% of the mediumship sessions I have delivered over the years, information "comes through" that the client knows absolutely nothing about. In most of those cases, the sitter ends up e-mailing me with validation that could not be validated during the session because they had no knowledge of the information at the time.

For example, I was once having a mediumship session with a woman named Tammy, and I kept receiving the name, "Milton." She could not figure it out even though the "signal" was strong. We kept coming back to that name over and over throughout the entire session, but we never figured it out during the appointment. Less than one week later, Tammy e-mailed me to confirm that, unbeknownst to her, her paternal grandfather's middle name was – you guessed it – Milton. It was his middle name, so she never knew that until she researched her family tree after our session. If it were one or two times that this happened, you could chalk it up to coincidence or luck. I am not kidding you when I tell you that this kind of situation has happened thousands of times. Because of these experiences, I can only reasonably conclude that I am not "reading the sitter's mind" during a session.

One of the most common claims that skeptics accuse mediums of is something called "cold reading." Cold reading is when a medium uses clues from the sitter, like facial reactions, body language, and subtle nonverbal clues to give the illusion to the client that they are receiving a great mediumship session. *Does this happen?* Unfortunately, I believe there are some frauds out there who do exactly this. However, there are many mediums who do not do this at all. Genuine mediums *do not want* that type of information, because it can significantly reduce the quality of a session. Mediumship sessions can be quite awkward at times because I will often look anywhere but directly at the client because I don't want any information in this manner. If the client has a reaction, it is easy to see or sense information from them, and that can be *very* distracting. Therefore, I try to avoid looking at the client as much as I can, to limit observing some of those natural reactions. Mediumship sessions are significantly better when I don't make too much eye contact with the sitter while obtaining information from the spirit world.

During a five-person blind mediumship certification I completed, not only could the client simply answer "yes," or "no," but I could not see them because most of those sessions took place over the phone or via Internet chat with no visual of the sitter. I enjoy phone mediumship sessions slightly better than in-person sessions because I cannot visually see anything that might throw me off. So, as much as skeptics want to accuse mediums of "cold reading," those "clues" are actually a significant detriment and quite a distraction to a genuine medium during a session. (You can view my mediumship certification here: https://www.findacertifiedmedium.com/mediums/ny/geneva/daniel-john/).

There are many times during a mediumship session that the information spirit is providing me doesn't line up with what the client is saying. One time I was having a session with a woman whose mom was coming through. The mother in spirit was telling me that their relationship was rocky at times. The woman refused to acknowledge this and said that she and her mom were close as could be. No offense to the sitters in my sessions, but I always listen to spirit because they are always right. As it turned out, my client held a lot of guilt about her relationship with her mom. She convinced herself that all was good, when in reality, she felt much guilt about the times that she and her mother "butted heads." After the woman finally admitted the guilt, through many tears, her mom came through to tell her to drop the guilt of those times because the great times significantly outweighed the "bad" ones. Spirit is so magical and undoubtedly healing.

Another common claim that skeptics accuse mediums of is that the medium used social media or some type of search engine to obtain specific, accurate information about the client. There are probably some "mediums" who do this, and that is unfortunate. As for me and many other genuine mediums, this claim is actually quite humorous. To the skeptic's credit, when I went to my first mediumship session – as a true skeptic – I thought there was a possibility that the medium did exactly that. However, the truth is that most of the information that comes through in a mediumship session is not able to be found anywhere on the Internet. As well, with three children, having a full-time day job, being a spiritual teacher, and as the president of a nonprofit organization, not only would I never even think of doing such a thing, I also simply don't have time for that. There are occasions however, when some information I must relay, *can* be found online. It is not very often, however, as 90+% of the information that comes through during a mediumship session is very specific, very accurate, and extremely meaningful to the client. And it is nowhere to be found online.

There have been many skeptics who have tried to debunk some of the most well-known mediums with limited success. *Are there mediums out there who 'cheat?'* Probably. However, I strongly feel that most mediums are not only practicing mediumship for the right reasons, but they are also actually communicating with the spirit world in order to help others, especially those who are grieving. I was a huge skeptic about mediumship until I experienced it myself. Having an open mind is so important when it comes to mediumship and in all areas of life as well.

Some skeptics claim that mediums just give very general information that could apply to many people. This claim may seem quite reasonable, because there are times when basic information like, "I love you," or, "I am okay," does come through. However, most of the time, that "general" information is exactly what the client needs to hear. Recently, I was having a mediumship session with a client named Brenna, and her mother was coming through with such force and with so much love. I told Brenna that I knew, "I love you," was a basic message that almost everyone could probably validate, but this is what her mom was telling me to tell her. Brenna broke into tears, raised her arm into the camera, and showed me a tattoo she received in memory of her mother that literally read "I love you." The tattoo was from a note her mother wrote her when she was little. This was her mother's way to acknowledge the tattoo, and at the same time validate her eternal love, as well as demonstrate her constant presence in her daughter's life.

Three simple common words can provide so much healing and validation. Most of the time however, the information that comes through in a session is very specific to the client, and most times, it is validated beyond comprehension. I don't question what I receive from spirit because I trust the universal energy of Love/Spirit 100%. Love is never wrong. Mediums are simply a conduit or instrument that spirit uses to express information to a person here on Earth.

Once I was having a session with a client, and I was told to say the name, "Bob," or "Robert." Not only is that a common name, but the client insisted she didn't know anyone by that name. Spirit insisted, however. I was persistent with the information I was receiving because most of the time the client needs a little time to think. After about two minutes, when the sitter could not figure out the name, I asked spirit for permission to move on. I assume I was granted permission from spirit to say another name, so I told her what I was receiving. The spirit immediately gave me the name, "Ellie," or "Eleanor." The next words out of my client's mouth still make me laugh as I write this.

She said, "That is funny, Daniel. My best friend passed away a few months ago, and her name was 'Ellie Bob.''

Why her friend in spirit started with her last name, is just one small example of how spirit communicates in a very different fashion than one would expect. This is the exact reason why most skeptics/cynics will remain in their disbelief of spirit communication. The experiences I have had – many that I will share in the following pages – are often beyond logic and comprehension. Spirit is always powerful, accurate, magical, and most of all, full of love.

Another common accusation that skeptics and cynics make about mediumship is that mediums simply toss out information until they get some validation. This would be a reasonable accusation if the medium kept giving information that was not validated until they "get a hit." Most of the mediumship sessions I have witnessed, including what I have experienced from my own sessions, illustrate that although there is information that is not validated during the session, 80% to 90% of the information is almost immediately validated by the sitter. Also, the medium sticks with that information until the client can understand what the medium is trying to relay. If you are watching or visiting a medium and they just keep throwing out message after message with no validation, and then once they "hit" something, they dwell on it and illustrate their validation, that may be a red flag that the medium just might be a charlatan or a phony.

Another misconception about mediumship – two-way communication with the deceased – is that mediums are evil, and they are communicating with "the devil." Over the years, I have had a few people e-mail or direct message me to tell me that what I am doing is wrong, it's "demonic," and that I am not communicating with passed loved ones, but with some evil entity who is trying to harm me and/or my client. If you would like an in-depth explanation of this, please refer to Chapter 6 in my first book. I will give a top-line explanation about this here as well.

Even though I have received some e-mails from people who think mediumship is "demonic" or "wrong," in the past, it used to cause me to question what I was doing. It took me many books, a lot of praying, and a lot of trust in God to help me understand that what I am doing as a medium is actually a gift from God and not some "evil spirit fooling me." For some reason these accusers seem to think they know more about my role as a medium than I do, because of what *they believe* the Bible says.

Without getting fully into Chapter 6 in my first book, here is what I have to say about this: I am quite familiar with the Bible. I read it daily, and I have also read many books about how to best use/read the Bible. I use the Bible as a tool to spread love, not fear. The Bible has taught me how I believe God wants me to live my life. Whether you read the Bible, the *Quran*, the *Bhagavad Gita*, or any other Holy book, it is up to you what you want to believe and how you want to live your life. In my opinion, the only universal truth is love. I will cover more about this topic in Chapter 7 in this book as well.

If you are grieving and would like to visit a medium to connect to your loved ones, but your religion or other people try to tell you that seeking out a medium is "wrong," or "demonic," I encourage you to pray about it. As a result, you will receive significant feelings or signs to direct you one way or another, and you will know if visiting a medium is a good idea for you. Trust, and pay attention to what God, The Universe, you, or your higher self/Love, thinks is best for you in your life. It is better to listen to your own heart/intuition when making decisions about your life as opposed to listening to what others think is best for you. Be yourself and trust what the Universe is guiding you to do. (Galatians 1:10).

I have been called a "Bible thumper" by some in the psychic community and I have been called "the devil" by some "Christians," but I am going to continue to do what I firmly believe God is instructing me to do. I have been called a "scam artist," "a fraud," and some other unfavorable things from those who simply don't understand what I do, but it only strengthens my passion to spread more love and to continue to be true to myself and to God, so I may be of service to others. Thankfully, approximately 99% of the communications I receive from others are positive, appreciative, and so full of love. Please be true to yourself no matter what anyone else thinks. The sooner you realize that you have a very specific, unique purpose and mission here on Earth, and you let nothing, and no one, stop you from accomplishing that, the more beautiful life becomes.

CHAPTER 4

A DAY IN THE LIFE OF A MEDIUM

As I write this, I am in my early forties with a beautiful wife and three amazing children, ages 9, 7, and 5. We live in a small town in Upstate New York, and I've been a full-time medical sales representative for over eighteen years. Many people ask me what it's like to "be a medium," so I am going to dedicate this chapter to help answer that very valid question. The short answer to that question is that it doesn't really affect my life the way many people think it might. The deeper answer to that question is as follows:

Being able to connect to the spirit world is a beautiful thing that we are *all* capable of doing. There is no better feeling than being able to connect someone with the energy of their passed loved one, thereby supplying them very specific information that truly helps the grieving person heal. This experience will often allow the sitter to enjoy a more peaceful life. But what I do as a medium is so much more than that.

To put it simply, I pass on messages from "spirit," or "the Holy Spirit" (that is what I call It), to help people on their journey through life. In my opinion, information from the spirit world is available to all, and is accessible to all via simple prayer. However, due to grief and some of the limitations we put on ourselves, we can often block this energy/information.

When this whole "spiritual process" started for me back in 2017, I was instructed by spirit to stop gambling. I was instructed to stop watching pornography in 2018, and then in 2021, I was informed by spirit that I was to never drink to excess again. I know this may sound weird to many people but giving up some of the things I enjoyed was a sacrifice I was willing to make, because it better equipped me to serve God and others through mediumship. I don't really miss the porn or the alcohol, but I do miss playing Texas Hold 'Em. I really enjoyed that. However, I would rather connect a grieving mother to the energy of her child who passed away suddenly in a car accident, than to shuffle some poker chips and win (or lose) a few bucks at the casino. There is nothing better than experiencing the magical healing that takes place during a mediumship session with a grieving person. It is beyond rewarding and it is simply pure, unconditional love.

Many of the things we do in this world, like the things I mentioned I had to quit, lower our vibration, and therefore, can limit us from accessing the universal omnipresent guidance from spirit. We are all connected to "Source," but unless we nurture ourselves and limit our egoic/human distractions, we can simply be blocked from Divine guidance.

Since 2017, I have made it a top priority to take care of myself energetically in order to maintain a high vibration so I can serve others. As mentioned, I don't get drunk, gamble, or watch pornography. I meditate and pray daily. I eat properly, exercise as much as I can, show kindness to others, consistently forgive, and do not judge others for anything. These conscious activities raise my vibration so I can better connect to the spirit world. You can also do the same.

Throughout a normal day for me, it is rare for spirit to randomly intercede other than in the form of my own daily intuitive guidance. Mediumship that I provide for others simply happens when God needs it to. It is not something I can control, but I trust that when I get information to pass on to help someone, it is what needs to happen. I used to question spirit communication all the time, but I have learned to trust in God and in His Divine guidance. There have been many times when I have been prompted by spirit to pass on a message while in public, but that is not a daily thing. Ninety-five percent of the time, I live a "normal" life with limited "interference" from the spirit world.

When I do receive a message to pass on to someone while in public, I am *extremely* calculated as to how, when, and even *if* I deliver it. In Chapter 6, I will cover the ethics of being a medium, but I will share a few basic rules I follow when spirit "pops through" unexpectedly.

The very first thing I do when this happens is question the spirit. I know that sounds funny, but because spirit communication is so subtle for me, I must make sure I am not fabricating random thoughts in my head. Spirit communication is that subtle most times and I describe it as just coming in like a thought. Remember, I don't "see" spirit with my eyes, or "hear" spirit with my ears. Spirit communicates with me through my thoughts. That is the best way I can describe it. Once I confirm that "it's happening," I ask spirit for the information that they want me to pass on to the receiver of the message. At this point, it still feels like a complete fabrication in my mind. When I approach the person, it is often awkward. What am I supposed to say, "Hey, I have your dead Grandma here and she wants to tell you something?" It can be quite uncomfortable.

As a medium, it is essential to remember that some people are not open to this sort of thing and some people actually think spirit communication is "wrong," or "evil," based on their experiences or beliefs. Since that is the case, I must be very careful about what I do as a medium in a public setting. I usually say something like, "Are you open to receiving a message?" or "Can I share something with you?" If they oblige, I will tell them that I am a medium and I receive messages to pass on from spirit. Ninety percent of the time, people are open to it. I have had a few times, however, where the person says, "No," and in those cases I simply and sincerely wish them a great day.

Once I obtain verbal permission from the intended receiver, the floodgates are open. Information just pours through. Names, symbols, numbers, nicknames, and even song titles and lyrics. The amount of detailed specific information spirit shares is beyond amazing.

I do not know the future. I do not know the lottery numbers. I can't read your mind, and I don't know if you are going to get a job, find a new relationship, or move to a new house. I only obtain information that God wants me to receive, so I can pass it on to others who may not be able to obtain it themselves. It is that simple. I remember when I first pulled into the parking lot for my first session with a medium, I remember thinking, *Does she know I am here?* Mediumship doesn't work anything like that for me at all. To put it simply, I am just sensitive to energy. Because we do not die, and because we are all made of pure energy, I have the ability to connect with the souls of people who have left their physical body.

Other than passing on messages to loved ones here on Earth, I live an amazingly blessed life with limited "distraction" from the spirit world. I love playing with my children, listening to music, going on long walks, traveling, and hanging out with my wife. Most of my life has nothing to do with passing on messages from spirit. I would say I live a rather "normal" life overall, and I am so thankful and blessed for that.

CHAPTER 5

WHAT DOES THE WORD "PSYCHIC" ACTUALLY MEAN?

It is very important to remember when we use words to describe things, we are limiting the true deeper meaning and understanding of some very important concepts. There are a few definitions and descriptions of words I would like to cover, to help you better understand a little more about "spirit communication."

According to *Merriam-Webster Dictionary*, the word "psychic" is defined as: "Of or relating to the psyche," or "a person who is sensitive to nonphysical forces." *Oxford English Dictionary* (OED) states that the word "psychic" means: "Connected to strange powers of the mind that may not be able to be explained by natural laws." *Wikipedia* states that the word "psychic" is: "A person who claims to use extrasensory perception (ESP) to identify information hidden from normal senses, particularly involving telepathy or clairvoyance, or who performs acts that are apparently inexplicable by natural laws, such as psychokinesis or apportation." *Dictionary.com* states that "psychic" is: "Of or relating to the human soul or mind." To me, this last definition means that technically we are all "psychic."

With so many definitions, the word "psychic," has understandably been misunderstood for a very long time, so let's try to clear it up for everyone here and now. According to the combined definitions from the aforementioned sources, one could legitimately conclude that psychic information is information that is obtained by a human being without scientific explanation. Another way to put this is that when a human being obtains information without using any of the five senses (ESP), they are considered "psychic." "Psychic" doesn't mean someone knows all things, knows the future, or speaks to the dead. "Psychic" is a word that simply means "of the psyche/mind" or "supernatural." That's it. Over the years, it seems everyone has made their own definition of the word "psychic," and most of those descriptions are extremely inaccurate.

For some reason, a significant amount of people are actually scared of the word "psychic," as if it means something "bad" or "forbidden." Again, according to the definitions, "psychic" should have nothing to do with fear or evil because it is a natural part of who we are as souls. The best way to think of the word "psychic" is to think of it like an umbrella. "Psychic" is the umbrella that covers many different types of abilities that are beyond scientific explanation. Tarot card readers, fortune tellers, and mediums are all "psychic." *Why?* Because there is no scientific explanation as to how they receive their information. A psychic obtains information through extra-sensory perception (not using any of the five senses). There are many different types of "psychic abilities," but "psychic" is just the main word that covers what I believe Paul calls the "gifts of the spirit" that he mentions in his letter to the people of Corinth. (1 Corinthians 12:4-11). I feel that Paul is guiding us to use these "psychic" gifts to help others, and not to use them for evil or selfish reasons like desire for fame, greed, or to murder someone like Saul is believed to have done. (1 Samuel 28).

The reason I don't call myself a "psychic," even though technically all humans have psychic ability, is because people get so misled by the word. They think "psychic" means knowing the future, and that is simply not accurate at all. Fortune telling and predicting the future are a form of psychic ability, but a "psychic" may have other supernatural abilities and may not even be able to perform fortune telling, specifically. So, please remember as you read this book, "psychic" only means that one is receiving information from somewhere beyond the physical realm, without the use of any of the five senses, and there is no scientific explanation as to how they receive it. That's it.

I do not perform fortune telling sessions and I do not claim to know the future. Those are not my gifts. As a medium – I call myself a "spiritual medium" – I connect with spirit, and often the sitter's deceased loved ones, specifically, to pass on valuable, accurate, and helpful information to those who are grieving here in the physical world. If you are reading this book, and you want a "reading" from a "psychic," I am *not* your guy. If you would like a session with someone because you are grieving, therefore, you are looking to connect with your loved ones in spirit, you would like to increase your faith in God (or a higher being), and/or you are open to some general guidance from the spirit world, I could be your guy.

It seems like a thin line between getting some guidance and fortune telling, and I believe it is. The difference is in the nature of the intent. If you are looking for *specific* answers to questions you have, I personally believe you can obtain that information yourself from "God," or "your higher self," via prayer. If you want to connect with a passed loved one, you are looking for general spiritual guidance, and you are open to what spirit wants to share about your life, that is more in line with what I do.

I mention this in my first book, but as a medium, my purpose is to pass on messages from the spirit world to people here in the physical world. According to the *Oxford English Dictionary*, the word "medium," as a noun, is defined as "an agency or means of doing something," or "the intervening substance through which impressions are conveyed to the senses." As an adjective, *Oxford* states that the word "medium" means "about halfway between two extremes." According to *Merriam-Webster Dictionary*, as a noun, "medium" is defined as either "something in a middle position," or "a middle condition or degree." As an adjective, *Webster* defines "medium" as "a means of effecting or conveying something such as a channel or system of communication, information, or entertainment."

Any human being who is able to receive and pass on a message from your deceased Aunt Edna, Archangel Michael, and yes, even Jesus, is a medium. We all can receive messages from "spirit." One can reasonably conclude, after reading Matthew 28:20, that Jesus is telling us he is "always with us." How do you think Paul, who is believed to have scribed approximately half the New Testament, obtained all the information he scribed? *You guessed it.* He obtained it "psychically." I personally feel it would be accurate to say that Paul was inspired by the Holy Spirit. According to Scripture, Jesus was not "in a physical body" when Paul was accomplishing his ministry. How was Paul getting his information from Jesus if Jesus wasn't "alive" or in a physical body?

Yup. . . Paul was a medium who channeled information from the spirit world. (Galatians 1:11-12). Paul was a "medium" between the spirit world and the physical world. And mediums can get that same type of divine guidance to this very day.

Many ancient cultures and even some current religions consistently communicate with the spirit world. I believe the spirit world communicates with human beings on a regular basis even though we often can't "see" it or "prove" it. The amount of anecdotal evidence that illustrates the reality of spirit communication is quite overwhelming. However, there seems to be some fear and discouragement in certain religions regarding communicating with the spirit world, especially here in the West.

In my opinion, there is a web of beautifully designed "Love" we are forever connected to, that is accessible to us when "God' wants it to be. When we look beyond our human existence, there is an infinite universe that we are eternally part of, that is more expansive than we can even begin to comprehend. This is why I believe many of Jesus' teachings are in the form of parables and analogies. We are simply not programmed to understand our true lives as spirit because we are so attached to the ego (the human body), and to what we perceive to be reality. There is a plethora of extremely useful spiritual information available to us as human beings if we are simply able to trust in something greater than our human minds can imagine. *Ask and you shall receive*. (Matthew 7:7).

When you see someone advertise themselves as a "psychic medium," there is really no need to preface the word "medium" with the word "psychic," because it is already implied. All mediums are "psychic." All fortune tellers and tarot card readers are "psychic," because there is no scientific law that explains how they receive their information. When you are walking in New York City, for instance, and you see a store with a neon red sign in the window that says, "Psychic," you are grammatically and semantically correct if you walk in and ask, "What kind of psychic are you?" or "What do you specialize in?"

Isn't it crazy that one word can be so misleading? One letter, one punctuation mark, and even one misunderstood definition or translation, can change the whole meaning of a story, a sentence, or even a simple word. In Chapter 7, you will see how different interpretations of words and teachings can cause some confusion on how to best interpret Scripture.

CHAPTER 6

THE ETHICS OF MEDIUMSHIP

Communication with spirit is not a game, party trick, or some sort of magical illusion. Mediumship sessions are a delicate, intimate, and complicated process. They are an emotional reunion between people here in the physical world and the energy/soul of loved ones who have returned Home to our natural state as "spirit," or to put it another way, "pure energy," who have no need for a physical body. Proper mediumship work – and it is work – is a major responsibility that takes time, energy, patience, and unconditional love to perform. Millions of people over the years have depended upon mediums to communicate messages from their loved ones who have passed away. These types of reunions, can, and often do, rekindle the flame of life that is often extinguished when one experiences the physical loss of a loved one. There can be a significant amount of pressure to ensure I get my clients the information their loved ones in spirit would like to communicate to them.

There are many things to be conscious of while communicating with the spirit world. In my opinion, it is not safe to practice mediumship without taking the proper precautions and educating yourself on best practices. I teach classes about understanding energy and mediumship development so I can help my students guide others who may need some sort of assistance. I would like to share with you a small glimpse of what I teach my students about the ethics behind mediumship. The reason I teach these classes is because mediumship is a very intricate process that requires the proper amount of very specific sets of circumstances to be effective, such as pure intent, passion, ethics, and pure unconditional love.

The single most important thing to highly consider before communicating with the spirit world is to pray and protect yourself. From my experience, I strongly believe that prayers work, and that protection is imperative. Because of the relative ambiguity of spirit communication, we really don't *know* for an absolute fact who and/or what we are communicating with. The only reason I have concluded that I am communicating specifically with the souls of people who have passed away is because of the overwhelming amount of specifically validating, evidentiary, healing, and loving messages that I have been able to pass on to thousands of grieving loved ones here on Earth.

Protection is a pretty simple process overall. I start and end every session with a protection prayer to God, to the angels, and to my spirit guides. With pure intention, I simply ask to be engulfed in God's White Light, while also asking Him to keep me and my client impervious from any "negative" energies that are not aware that they too are part of God's infinite, unconditional, eternal Love. Remember that your thoughts and intentions create your reality, so, as long as you are pure with those intentions, God's Light of Love is infinitely available to you. So, it is in everyone's best interest to use His/Her/Its' Light to spread His/Her/Its' Love.

Another important thing I teach my students is to trust the spirit world and to trust in the messages they receive from spirit. Remember, if your intention is pure – i.e., you're not practicing mediumship to make money, be famous, or to be a charlatan, the information you receive will not only be pure love, but it will be divinely guided by Source. Trust was the biggest hurdle I had to navigate when I first started practicing mediumship. As I've said, for me, messages from the spirit world are so subtle that it sometimes feels as though I am making it up. Even though spirit communication can sometimes feel extremely subtle and fabricated, when you trust that the information is coming from somewhere Divine, it can become very accurate, extremely strong, and quite definitive. When I attended my first mediumship development class, it was quite apparent that once I trusted the signs and symbols I was receiving from spirit, the information was validated more than I could have imagined.

The last of the three main points I teach my students besides protection and trust, is to always ask permission from the person to whom they are to deliver a message. This is *so* important! Permission is implied when a sitter proactively books an appointment with a medium. There are cases, however, while in public or at an event, that the permission is not implied, and a medium must seek approval before delivering what they believe to be a message from the spirit world. Not everyone is willing, able, or ready to receive and accept such a message.

Our loved ones in spirit know what is best for us, but because our ego-based reality can often make us feel like we are separate from God, or the Whole, we may not believe we are ready. Some may think they are ready to receive communication from their loved ones in spirit, but spirit knows we are not. Unless I receive permission from the person for whom a message is intended, I refuse to fulfill the request of a loved one in spirit. I could count on one hand the number of times I have received a message from spirit, and then asked for permission from the proposed sitter, and was denied permission. It is imperative, however, to get approval from the intended receiver in order to be able to deliver a meaningful message from the spirit world.

Here are some things that are standard protocols during my mediumship sessions:

I keep my prices very reasonable and donate 50% of my earnings from private sessions to the nonprofit organization, *Heaven for the Homeless*.

I record every single session and e-mail it to my clients the same day or the next day after the appointment. I am consciously aware that it is highly probable that the person who booked a session with me is severely grieving. Therefore, I must exercise compassion for the sitter before, during, and after every single session. I am a naturally compassionate person, so that's a plus.

I always go over the one hour allotted time for the appointment to honor everyone involved in the session. I listen to direction from God/Spirit and my spirit guides on when to end a session. I have gone over two hours at times because that is what the client needed, and I did not charge them a penny more than the original booking price.

In the approximately four years I have been a practicing medium, there have been only three times where the session was a "dud," and nothing validating came through. I refunded two of them. The other session where nothing came through was for a woman named Charity. Her husband had passed away, but he visited her in a dream the night before her session to tell her he would not be coming through in her appointment with me. She didn't tell me that information until I was struggling to get any validating messages. I offered her a refund about halfway through her appointment, but she instructed me to donate her session to another person. I did, and that session was absolutely beautiful. And by the way, how fitting is it that this woman's name is "Charity?" If that isn't crazy enough, all the information that came through in Charity's session was extremely validating information for a good friend of mine named Jackie. Jackie's high-school sweetheart used the opportunity to come through from the other side to express his never-ending love for her in a *very* specific way. All the messages Charity did not validate were later validated by Jackie.

Over the years, I have learned many things that are important to consider, whichever side of the table you sit at during a mediumship session. I am a big believer in constructive criticism, and I love making myself better every single day. It sometimes takes an uncomfortable conversation in order to grow and learn. I have been blessed enough to have had some of these conversations with some amazing people who were willing to get a little uncomfortable in order to help me improve my capabilities as a medium. I want to share a few of these improvements I have made to my sessions over the last few years in order to be the most effective channel of God's eternal and unconditional Love:

While conducting a session with a soul who crossed over by suicide, I will use the words, "took their own life," or "they are taking responsibility for their own passing," as opposed to "committed suicide." It turns out that some people who are left here in the physical world prefer not to use or hear the latter phrase while speaking about their loved one who passed in such a manner.

During a session, any time I come to understand of a loved one's passing, I make it a point to say, "I am sorry for your loss." I don't just say it. I truly mean it. I have watched way too many mediums, myself included, get so caught up in the excitement of a validation or connection, that they forget to exercise any sort of compassion for the sitter. That is just my personal style. I am not saying any other medium is wrong for doing what they do in whatever way they do it.

One of the most difficult things I must do is to tell a client that they misunderstood a message from their loved one. Once, I was having a session with a woman and her deceased mother wanted me to "talk about the bracelet." As soon as I communicated her mother's message, the daughter immediately broke into tears, got emotional, and responded, "Oh, my God, I am wearing Mama's rings." Now, I know her mom was not talking about the rings her daughter was wearing, but instead, her mom specifically wanted to talk about "the bracelet." When it comes to jewelry, I ask spirit to be *very* specific with the type of piece and location, because jewelry is a very common thing to "talk about" or "pass down." I uncomfortably had to tell my client that was not what her mom was talking about, and I restated her mother's message about the bracelet. It turns out that my client's sisters had all made bracelets in honor of their mom, and the sitter forgot that she had just received hers in the mail the week before the session.

To put it bluntly, as a medium, I sometimes must pass on information that can be very basic and therefore applies to many people, seems just plain silly, and/or is wildly inappropriate. I don't try to appease the skeptics, but there are many times I must tell a sitter a basic message like their loved one is, "okay on the other side," or I must pass on a simple, "I love you." As a former skeptic myself, I love the very specific validations, but I have learned over the years that even though messages may sound generic and/or I don't understand the meaning behind the messages, they are always very meaningful. I always honor spirit because they know significantly more than we do.

I also want you to know that there is absolutely no competition in the genuine mediumship world. We all work for God, and the grieving person will find and connect with the medium they are supposed to sit with. I have met many great mediums over the years who have pure intentions and simply want to help others connect with their loved ones in spirit. I cannot tell you how many times I have recommended one of my many medium friends or former students to someone who was looking for a mediumship session with me. I always let spirit guide me to guide others in whatever way God/Spirit wants me to do so.

I do everything within my power to ensure my clients get the information that will serve their highest good. Many times, the clients won't know what's best for themselves as much as spirit does, because many human beings get lost in the ego and Earthly things. (Colossians 3:2). Many of those who are grieving are not as in touch with the Divine Love that resides in each and every single person on this Earth. I feel it is my job to remind people that they are eternally connected to an Unconditional Eternal Love (God), whether they realize it or not.

I want to end this chapter by telling you something I will say just a few times in this book. You do not need someone who says they are a "medium" to connect with "spirit" or your loved ones who have passed away. You can connect with spirit all on your own. The reason I do what I do is because all too often, the grieving miss their loved ones so much, they sometimes lose their faith in God. Unfortunately, it is common for most people to operate at a low vibration when they lose a loved one. This is due partly to the grief they experience, but it can also be a result from some of the other "negative" influences that exist in this world. I am here to restore faith in something greater than we can even imagine. The word we most commonly use is "God," but that word does not do justice to the Eternal Love that we are all infinitely part of and are connected to. You are a spark of that Divine Whole. I personally believe that our true lives are in spirit form as energy, and that energy is eternal. As energy, we cannot be created or destroyed. As Jesus showed us, when we "die," we just change form, but we live forever. (Mark 16:12). We do not die, and your loved ones who have passed away are still with you, literally.

CHAPTER 7

MEDIUMSHIP AND CHRISTIANITY

I covered part of this topic in my first book, but because a different type of audience may read *this* book, I did not want to leave out such a big part of my life especially when it relates to the world's most followed religion. Please read Chapter 6 in my first book to get a full, unbiased look at religion as a whole and how it relates to mediumship. There, I cover a wide range of helpful information that is not included in this book.

I was raised Catholic and attended a Catholic elementary school from kindergarten through sixth grade. I taught Catholicism in college even though I was "saved" as a Christian in ninth grade. Now, as a forty-two-year-old man, when anyone asks me what religion I am, I simply tell them my religion is "Love." For me, "Love" is the best word in the English language that describes the theme of my life and where/what I believe we "come from" and "return to."

I conduct my life with love, compassion, forgiveness, equality, non-judgement, and kindness. I believe in Jesus, and I feel that he was a human being who best represented our Source. I believe in God, but I do not think we can define Him/Her/It. I believe what most people call "God," is beyond our understanding and language. 1 John 4:8 says, "God is Love," but I feel that even the word, "Love," truly doesn't do "It" any justice. The best analogy/definition I use to describe what most people call "God," is that He/She/It is "the ocean of everything," or "the sum of all the parts." I believe that you and I are a part of the Greater Whole that most people call "God." I believe that each and every one of us contains a drop of the ocean we call "God" (the soul). Altogether, we make up "God." In 1 John 10:30-34, when Jesus talks about his divinity and comparison to "God," the Pharisees want to stone him. "Is it not written in your law, 'I have said you are gods?'" (1 John 10:34). (NIV).

I do not believe that God is a man in the sky with a staff and rod who judges us and either condemns us to an "eternal hell" or approves select people to enter a place some people call "Heaven." To me, that is dogma. I also personally don't believe in an eternal hell. Again, for me, dogma. I believe in "Heaven" and "hell," but I believe they are words used to describe a state of mind, not a permanent place we either earn a spot in or get condemned to, respectively.

My beliefs are based on many books about near-death experiences, mediumship, religious books – including the Bible – and thousands of sessions with clients in which I directly connect to the spirit world. If your beliefs are different from mine, that is awesome, and I love you just the same. I used to try to get people to believe what I believe, but I would often find myself in many uncomfortable conversations. One person would try to convince the other that they were right. Now, I embrace all beliefs and all religions, and I do not judge anyone or try to change them.

I don't believe that one religion is more correct than another. I encourage you to obtain that same sense of peace when it comes to religion, politics, or anything else. To each their own! You will be a lot less stressed when you stop trying to convince other people of what you believe to be "right" or "true," and you just accept that everyone else has their own opinions and beliefs. To each their own! *Yes, I just repeated that.*

I personally do not believe that Jesus was God alone, or that he is "the only Son of God," as it states in John 3:16. I do, however, believe that Jesus is a child of God just like you and me. In my opinion, Jesus personified the type of person who most represents Love (God). I look at Jesus like a big brother and as someone who is a guide, as opposed to someone who "died for our sins" or who is "God himself."

Now again, I do believe that Jesus represents the Divine in human form, but I do not feel that he is God himself singly. In my opinion, I feel when someone states that Jesus is God, they are disregarding the second commandment. "Only God is God." (Mark 10:18). Both John 14:12 and 1 Corinthians 11:1 state that we are guided to "be like Jesus," and we should do the works he does and more. In my opinion, these verses suggest that we are to strive to be just like Jesus, and that we can perform all the miracles he did. How are we able and encouraged to mimic Jesus' ways without being part of "God" or "children of Him" ourselves? (Romans 8:14).

As a point of understanding for the reader, please note that I do not capitalize the "H" in "him" when referring to Jesus, because, as I said, I think God is God and Jesus is Jesus and not God alone. (Mark 10:18). We simply must find that divinity (Christ/Love) within ourselves in order to connect to our Source on the highest level. . .pure Love, just as Jesus was able to do.

Now that you have an idea of where I stand in my beliefs when it comes to God, Jesus, and the Bible, I hope that you can still appreciate and respect my opinion, even though you may or may not have similar beliefs as I do about those things. I have some Muslim and Buddhist friends, and even though we have different beliefs, customs, and rituals, we are still friends. My friends and I can still chat about our different beliefs without trying to convince the other to change their mind or disrespect each other for what each of us believes. I have this sense of acceptance with strangers too, and I hope you can get to that point one day if you aren't there already.

It took me many years to understand that just because I believe certain things, especially when it comes to religion, that doesn't mean I am right, or that everyone must believe what I believe. They are called "beliefs" instead of "truths" for a reason.

There are certain "Christians" who were taught at some point in their lives that mediumship is "demonic," or "from the devil," or that "God doesn't approve of mediums." Let me help you understand that, again, this is rhetoric and dogma, and this misunderstanding stems from lack of knowledge, ignorance, fear, and unfortunate misinterpretation of Scripture.

Once in a great while I receive an e-mail or message from someone who claims to be a "Christian," who either accuses me of performing the work of the devil or tells me that "God will punish me for forsaking Him." They tell me I need to "repent" and "stop doing the devil's work immediately." This is an example of coming from a place of ignorance and fear. As I mentioned previously, 99% of the messages and e-mails I receive are full of love, compassion, and gratitude for my work, and I am extremely thankful for that. I do, however, want to share with you why I firmly believe that what most genuine mediums do is not only a spiritual gift from God, but that the use of their gift is often part of the medium's life purpose in service to Him and to others.

There are a handful of Scriptures in the Torah, or the Old Testament, that can lead one to believe, and quite reasonably so, that mediumship was something that was discouraged in ancient Israel when these texts were written. There are verses that lead the reader to believe that mediumship is discouraged in Deuteronomy, Leviticus, Samuel, and even in Kings. When I was first reminded of these verses in the Hebrew Bible, I reread them, and quickly decided to stop practicing mediumship. That thought only lasted about five seconds until I was reminded of the peace, compassion, forgiveness, and absolute pure love that I had experienced in *all* my mediumship sessions up to that point.

To say that I was torn, would be an understatement. *How could I have experienced all these powerful connections and witnessed an abundance of amazing healings and Divine guidance if this communication with the spirit world was "the devil," or "demonic," and therefore not supported by God?*

For those who think the Bible is the absolute word of God with no flaws and no room for interpretation, I cannot help them understand. For those who have cognitive dissonance because of what has been burned into their minds from either their church or from reading Scripture in a black and white fashion without looking at the context and meaning of each verse, I can't help them understand what I do as a medium either. What I can offer, however, to those who are open-minded enough, is an explanation of how mediumship has proved to be one of the most beautiful experiences I have ever had. The ability to connect with the spirit world is absolutely natural, and it is also something that would not be possible without "Source," or "The Divine," or something most of us call "God."

If you pick up a Bible and read a verse without looking at why, where, who, and when the text was written, I don't think that is the best way to learn from Scripture. I use the Bible as a guide to help me spread God's unconditional love for all. I personally think that love is the original intent for the Bible, and for any other Holy book, for that matter. So, before I go into my explanation of why I believe that mediumship is a gift from God, when you read the Bible, please read it with love. Please don't use it to change anyone based on your beliefs and the way you interpret Scripture. In my opinion, everyone will read and interpret Scripture differently and that is perfectly okay. Are you using the love in your heart when you make a decision, take an action (read Scripture, for example), or have a thought? That is what it's all about. The way you live your life is not about "how," it's not about "where," it's not about "who," and it's not even about what you do. The only thing that truly matters is your "why." Your intention is the main aspect of anything you think, say, or do. (1 Corinthians 13:2-3). It's not about what you believe. All that matters is how you love.

In the handful of Scriptures people use to judge and condemn mediumship, one must look more deeply into the text. As I mentioned earlier, the "anti-mediumship" verses are *all* in the Torah or Old Testament. These "laws" were written well over 2,000 years ago in ancient Israel by people who lived in a very different culture and at a very different time. Not only are there some pretty disturbing laws and rules written back then (Deuteronomy 21:18-21), but the people of that time seemed to have some very confusing, extreme, and different beliefs about "God," animal and human sacrifices, and communication with the dead, among many other things.

Some accusers will even use the story of Saul in the Old Testament to support damning mediums when they unfortunately aren't looking at the context and deeper meaning of the story. Was God mad at Saul for seeking out a medium? I believe so. But again, you must understand the context and circumstances around the situation. According to Scripture, Saul was looking to murder David. Saul banned all mediums in the land and then selfishly and secretively consulted one. Saul used a "medium" to communicate with spirit for personal gain and evil doing.

According to Scripture, Saul didn't consult a medium because he missed his mom, or his child died, and he wanted to make sure they were alive and with God. Saul was a murderer, and he sought a medium to conduct evil. The translators of the Bible even use the term, "Witch of Endor," when referring to the medium Saul is believed to have consulted, just to further ingrain the fear of communication with the spirit world. The Hebrew word used to describe this woman is, "ba'alat ov," which more literally translates to "communicator of the familiar spirit," not "witch," which can sometimes connote negative impressions. (You can reference the Oxford English Dictionary's definition of the word "witch").

In my opinion, seeking out a medium, with pure intentions, to connect with a loved one in spirit so you can live your life in a fulfilling way is absolutely okay. I firmly believe mediumship is one of the best forms of grief counseling that one can experience. To this very day, there are many churches who host mediums during their services which are intended to guide and support the grieving.

Most theologians and biblical scholars agree that most of the writers of the Hebrew Bible had a very inconsistent view of the afterlife. One could assume after reading Old Testament Scripture, that there doesn't seem to be a uniform belief among the Jews regarding thoughts and beliefs about what the afterlife entails. They often talk about a place called "Sheol," which in Hebrew refers to "the place of the dead." One can even conclude that some writers of the Old Testament did not believe in an afterlife at all, or that some writers believed that the departed rested until the day of judgement. (Hebrews 9:27). It is also important to note that the Egyptians, who were neighbors to the Israelites, spent a significant amount of time and money attempting to preserve the human body after death in the form of mummies.

Most Christians follow the teachings of Jesus. A "Christian" is someone who follows Christ. Jesus's name was "Yeshua," which is the Hebrew name of "Joshua." And no, his last name wasn't "Christ." "Christ" is how many people refer to Jesus. The word "Christ" comes from the Greek word "Christos." In Greek, "Christos" means "the anointed one." When we find Christ within ourselves, we recall that we are naturally part of the "anointed One," and act accordingly by extending unconditional love for all. You, me, and everyone in this world are all part of the Divine, and Jesus led the way for Christians (and all others, for that matter), to find Christ/Love in ourselves. (John 14:12).

Here is the bottom line. . .

Now, please remember that earlier in this book, we defined "medium" as "the halfway point between two extremes." When it comes to mediumship specifically, it means communication between the spirit world and the physical/human world. Not only did Jesus *never once* speak negatively about mediumship anywhere in the Bible, but according to Scripture, he consistently demonstrated two-way communication with the spirit world.

In Matthew 17, Jesus and some of the apostles go up on a mountain and communicate with the departed Moses and Elijah. *That is exactly the definition of mediumship.* Mediumship is simply two-way communication with the spirit world.

The Bible is full of communication between the spirit world and our world. The Bible is a book that has more mediumship in it than any other book I can think of. When Ananias was "instructed by God" to heal Saul/Paul of his blindness (Acts 9:10-16), how do you think he received that information? You got it. He received it from spirit. Oh, by the way, don't forget, according to Scripture, Saul/Paul, the presumed writer of approximately half the New Testament, never met Jesus while Jesus was in body. Jesus had already been crucified by the time Saul/Paul "met" him. Doesn't that mean that Saul/Paul not only communicated with spirit (Jesus) on the road to Damascus, but that Jesus/The Holy Spirit/God/Spirit channeled messages through Paul both while he was in jail, and also when he was traveling to many different towns to preach? From where did Paul get his information? *You guessed it:* The spirit world. (Galatians 1:11-12). That makes Paul a "medium" between this world and the spirit world.

There is an amazing book written by Sydney Schwartz called "Mediumship in the Bible." In this book, Schwartz explains some errors the translators of the Bible made when constructing our modern Western Bible/canon. He demonstrates that the translators of the many versions of the Bible unintentionally, or possibly intentionally, severely mistranslated Scripture and misguided readers. If you read Schwartz's book, it will make you second-guess what the Bible writer's and translator's intentions were, especially when it comes to how each of them wanted the end user to understand Scripture as it relates to spirit communication.

If you are a Christian, and you were taught to believe that mediumship is "the devil," or "wrong," please relook at Scripture. I had to reread the Bible after I experienced the divine healing power of mediumship. Please, also remember that *never once* did Jesus speak against mediumship. *Not once.* Jesus was a medium and so was Paul. A medium simply connects the world here on Earth to the spirit world.

Acts 16:16 is another Scripture in the New Testament that some "Christians" use to judge and condemn mediumship. In this section of Acts, there was a slave owner who was using a woman's spiritual gifts to make himself money. This woman most likely did not want to be a slave, so, according to Scripture, she chased Paul and Silas around, bothering them until Paul, through the power of the Holy Spirit, removed her "psychic" abilities or "removed the evil spirits," because they were being used against her will and for sinful reasons. This is just one small example of how one can read Scripture out of context and therefore misunderstand the meaning behind the text.

Some others will use 1 John 4:1 to say that mediumship is "the devil," and I can't help but laugh. The verse is so much more accurate than most readers can even imagine. The verse states: "Beloved, do not believe every spirit, but test the spirits, because many false prophets have gone out into the world." (1 John 4:1). (NKJV). Some Christians will actually use this verse as a follow up to a verse from Leviticus or Deuteronomy, to judge and condemn mediums to some sort of "hell." *Oh, the ignorance*. In my opinion, John is saying to test the spirit of people you come in contact with, whether here in the physical world or in the spirit world. Spirit is spirit, whether in a human body or not.

Every physical body has a soul, the true spirit part of ourselves (Romans 8:15), whether you are a car salesman, a pastor, or a medium. There are some shady car salesmen out there, there are some pastors who have caused physical and sexual harm to others, and there are some mediums who are charlatans and scam people for money. *Does this mean that all car salesmen, clergymen, and mediums are evil? No.* It just means that some people are leading with fear and human desire (sin), as opposed to love and spiritual enlightenment. (Romans 8:12-13).

Just because John warns of false prophets, does that mean that all those who claim to have spiritual gifts are evil? Of course not. Does John warn us to be careful of with whom we interact and encourage us to protect ourselves from sinners, scammers, and those who don't have the best of intentions? In my opinion, absolutely. Just because the Holy Spirit spoke through John (oh, and by the way, that makes John a "medium" too), to warn us about false prophets, that does not mean that all people who claim to be prophets, or people who have spiritual gifts, are liars and are bad. Just test them with your intuition/heart.

If that isn't enough to make you think, please read 1 Corinthians 12:4-11 and 1 Peter 4:10 in the Bible. The same guy who "removed an evil spirit" in Acts 16, passes on a message from the Holy Spirit that states that each of us has unique special gifts from God that we are to use in our lifetime to assist others along their paths. Paul even mentions "prophecy" and "spiritual discernment" as "gifts of spirit." Yes, that means that fortune tellers and mediums with the best of intentions are utilizing their gifts from God to serve others.

So, if you are a Christian reading this book, and you were taught at some point that mediumship is wrong or against God, please reconsider. Misinterpretation of Scripture – not just from the Bible, but from other Holy books as well – has led to much conflict, persecution, war, and even death. Don't miss out on any opportunity to connect with your loved ones in spirit, connecting with angels, guides, or even connecting with Jesus on a spiritual level like St. Paul did.

Regardless of your beliefs and/or your religion, Jesus is always available to us. (Matthew 28:20). We, as humans, formed a religion with many branches around Jesus. According to Scripture, Jesus was anything but religious while he was incarnate. It was clear that Jesus was a voice for change among the Pharisees as he attempted to clear up any misinterpretation of ancient laws and customs during his incarnation. In my opinion, Jesus was a man who taught us to love all things unconditionally.

CHAPTER 8

WHAT IS GOD?

If you think you can define or understand what most people call, "God," I ask you to reconsider. If you ask one-hundred people to define "God," you will surely get one-hundred different answers. The reason I am including this chapter in this book is not to answer the question proposed in the title, but merely to let you know that it is okay to have your own interpretation on who and what "God" is. It is imperative that you recognize what most people call, "God," is indefinable and unable to be fully comprehended with our limited human minds. It is absolutely okay to conclude that "God" is, and always will be, a mystery to us as human beings.

In ancient and modern Israel, the word used to describe "God" is "YHWH." This word is so sacred and holy, most Jews believe the word is not to be spoken. *Merriam Webster's Dictionary* defines "God" as: "The perfect and all-powerful spirit or being that is worshiped by Christians, Jews, and Muslims as the One who created and rules the Universe." That surely isn't the real definition of "God," because, in my opinion, there is no definition for "God."

My personal interpretation of "God" is that God is the "Ocean of All Things." God is unconditional Love Itself. God is "It." He/She/It is literally the sum of all parts. You are part of "God." I am part of "God." Every grain of sand and particle in the entire infinite Universe equals "God." That is just my opinion, and perhaps your definition of "God" differs from mine. In whatever way you decide to try to understand our Creator/Source, and how you choose to serve others is up to you. Whatever religion you are part of and whatever rituals you practice is your choice. And, that freedom to do so, is one of the beautiful gifts (free will) that life offers us as human beings.

Being raised Catholic, I was taught to fear God, and I was afraid to be judged by Him. I was taught that church was the only way to experience anything Divine. I was taught to believe that "Heaven" is a place you go when you are good, and "hell" is a place you go when you are bad. I was taught that you must consult with a priest to ask for forgiveness, which will allow you to be accepted by God. I no longer believe this at all. If you believe in all or none of those things, that is totally okay. I believe we are supposed to have our own beliefs, and I also feel that each one of us has our own unique path in this world.

I was supposed to have those beliefs earlier in my life, but as I grew older, I was not to believe them anymore. And that is okay. Please be 100% okay with other people's beliefs when they differ from yours. We all have our own interpretations and our own lives to live. Let it be. There are over 4,000 religions in the world, and in my opinion, they are all perfect just the way they are, and each one serves its own unique purpose. At one point in my life, I was the guy who tried to get everyone to believe what I believed. As I became "enlightened," I realized that everyone believes what they need to believe at any particular time in their life. The more we accept others, the more peaceful the world will become. To each their own! (*Yes, I just said that again*).

I am a follower of Jesus and I read the Bible daily. That doesn't mean that *you* have to do either of those. I look at Jesus as one of many teachers who incarnated here on Earth to simply demonstrate who we truly are as souls, show us how we can be more connected to "God," and illustrate how we can vibrate as close as we can to the frequency of our Source (Love). I have many friends who are part of many different religions. I have friends who are agnostic, and I have some friends who are atheist. I *do not* try to change them. They are living their own beautiful lives with their own unique purposes. I believe there is only one universal truth and that is Eternal Unconditional Love.

I have come to accept all things, even the "bad" that happens in the world, because all things are always for the greater good whether we know it or not. (Jeramiah 29:11). There are some things in this world that most people would say, "There is no way any good can come out of this," or "Why would God allow such a thing?" I have come to understand and believe that since we are souls living in a human body, all experiences, including the "bad" or "negative" experiences we have, are always Divine. I firmly believe there is a bigger plan to all things, and when we recognize that the life we are currently experiencing is like a grain of sand in all of eternity, we are able to start to visualize a fractional glimpse of the bigger picture. All things are as they are and there are no mistakes. Even the things we cannot understand or comprehend are part of the plan. It's all about love because, in my opinion, God is literally Love Itself. (1 John 4:8).

CHAPTER 9

WHAT HAPPENS WHEN WE DIE? (HEAVEN OR HELL?)

The short answer to the question the title of this chapter asks is, "I don't know." However, since I have communicated with the spirit world for about four years, and I have read hundreds of books on near death experiences, mediumship, reincarnation, and theology, I can comfortably share with you what I have discovered.

As I mentioned in a previous chapter, I personally do not believe that "Heaven" and "hell" are places. I believe what some people call "Heaven" and what some people call "hell" are states of mind, or perception, not eternal, permanent destinations. Everyone has their own beliefs of the "afterlife," and I am not here to change yours, but here is what I have come to understand:

We all have a right to be in "Heaven," "Nirvana," or "Bliss," regardless of our religion or beliefs. We also have a right to be in the aforementioned state of being, whether we are physically in a human body or not. There is a part of you that is infinitely connected to the greater "Whole," or what most people call "God," or "The Universe." As we discussed earlier, this greater part of you is often called "the soul." According to *Merriam-Webster Dictionary*, the soul is defined as: "The spiritual part of a person that is believed to give life to the body and in many religions is believed to live forever."

71

I have come to understand a few basic principles about life after "death." One of the most common themes is that we are spiritual beings having a human experience. We do not die. We are energy, and at our core we are simply love. Don't forget what Einstein said: "Energy cannot be created or destroyed." We live forever. "Love" seems to be the best word besides, "spirit," that describes who we are as souls. Once you connect to that part of yourself (Christ or Love), which is who you truly are, you are more reflective of the Source you derived from. And don't forget, based on Scripture, that Source is simply "Love." (1 John 4:8). "Source," or "God," loves you more than you can even imagine because you are literally a piece of that Love. And yes, that Love means no "eternal hell," in my opinion.

If you asked me five years ago what a "near-death experience" (NDE) was, I probably would have looked at you like you had two heads. Ever since I started opening my heart and mind to things the Universe wanted me to understand more, I discovered there are many opportunities to learn about things I would have thought were "weird," or "dumb," or just "not real." NDEs are one of those things. It turns out there are millions – yes, millions – of people who have clinically died, and then returned to life. These experiencers claim to have significant amounts of information to share about the afterlife. At first, I thought these experiences may be attributed to hallucinations or dreams. However, as I continued to study ample amounts of NDE research and continued to read many books about NDEs, I started to understand that NDEs are a very real and extremely powerful experience for most people who claim to have had one.

A man by the name of Dr. Jeffery Long authored two books. One is called, "Evidence of the Afterlife: The Science of Near-Death

Experiences," and the other is called, "God and the Afterlife." In his books, Dr. Long breaks down the science of the NDE. Dr. Long has studied over 3,000 NDE subjects from many different cultures and religions. His general conclusion from years of extensive research is that there is significantly more depth to life than we can experience with our five senses and limited minds. Way more.

It wasn't until Dr. Raymond Moody coined the expression, "near-death experience" in 1975, that people started to attempt to understand what truly happens to people who clinically died and then returned to life. Many, but not all, "NDEers" (people who have reported having a near death experience/those who have clinically died and come back to life), experience profound feelings of love, compassion, "Heaven," and "Light." You can't even begin to wrap your head around what people who have had NDEs feel about their experiences until you read books like the ones I have mentioned, or until you watch YouTube® videos about NDEs. From all I have researched on NDEs, most experiences and experiencers are real, genuine, and come from the heart.

There is a significant amount of commonality among most people who have experienced a NDE, no matter their culture or background. Some of the common themes from my research and readings of NDEs are as follows:

- Meeting/communicating with passed loved ones

- A tunnel of extreme force, like a vortex

- Meeting with spiritual figures like Jesus

- Experiencing a greater understanding of their individual purpose on Earth

- Undergoing a life review

- An overwhelming feeling of love, compassion, comfort, warmth, and a sense of being "Home"

- Being told it is "not their time"

- Not wanting to "return" to Earth

I have come to understand what truly happens when we "die" can only be revealed to us when we each leave our physical bodies for the final time. However, I feel the research that Dr. Long and Dr. Moody have completed is essential to the spiritual community and to the world. "Life" is something exponentially bigger than we can see or even begin to understand. I know I haven't said it much, but I believe each one of us is part of "Eternity," or "God," or "the Universe." When we "die," we return "Home" to energy or spirit without the need for a physical body. We are energy and we cannot be created or destroyed. Life is eternal, as Jesus showed us, and as Dr. Long and Dr. Moody have concluded in their research as well. I encourage you to read some books about NDEs. The amount of anecdotal evidence showing that NDEs are real, and that they often have a significantly positive effect on the experiencer, is overwhelming.

I would like to take a deeper dive into some consistencies that my research of near-death experiences has revealed about what happens to us when our time comes to transition back to the spirit world.

The life review:

There is overwhelming anecdotal evidence that when we "pass away," we experience our entire life in one moment. We can experience, firsthand, how we affected other people throughout our last physical incarnation. Our soul can witness a 360-degree view of all our life experiences from every single angle. It is basically a review on how well we chose love, compassion, and forgiveness during our life, as opposed to choosing hatred, judgement, or fear. According to what I have experienced and read, our biggest judge is ourselves, not "God," or some jury that deems you worthy of "Heaven," or condemns you to an eternal "hell." It seems as though you are the main judge of your own life.

An overwhelming feeling of love:

Many NDEers have reported feeling loved more than they ever have been loved in their entire life on Earth. They feel what they can only describe as "pure unconditional love." Some NDEers have said that the word "love" just doesn't do justice to the emotional depth of their experience. They often describe a "warm light" or a "comforting embrace" that overwhelms them so much that they often cannot put the feelings into words. Many NDEers call this light, "Love."

Being greeted by loved ones:

An overwhelming number of NDEers report being in the presence of their loved ones who have passed before them. NDEers often recall being visited by family members, friends, and even Jesus. There have been tens of thousands of cases reported in which those on their deathbeds can visually see their passed loved ones right before they transition back to spirit ("die").

A new sense of life purpose:

One of the most electrifying results from many NDEs is that the experiencer "comes back" with a new passion for life that includes a significantly better understanding of their specific purpose/purposes here on Earth. Many NDEers wake up to newly discovered gifts of spirit they can use to help others. To me, Dr. Raymond Moody's invaluable research on NDEs is one of the most fascinating subjects. I think you may enjoy his work as well. If you have not read his book, "Life After Life," that sold over thirteen million copies, I highly recommend you read it.

Dr. Mary Neal was a spine surgeon who was kayaking in Chile when she died. Her NDE is one of the most compelling stories I have ever heard. She describes her experience in detail in her book, "Journey to Heaven and Back." Dr. Neal describes being enveloped in Christ's arms, experiencing a life review, viewing her body from a distance, and connecting with angels as she passed away to what she describes as "Home." Dr. Neal even claims that she was given a prophecy of the future passing of her son, and she claims she was also informed as to what her purpose was in experiencing such a painful reality.

New psychic gifts:

There have been thousands of reports of people who have developed psychic gifts after their NDE. These NDEers come back to Earth with many different kinds of gifts including clairaudience, clairvoyance, and mediumship abilities. NDE or not, if you have a gift you can use to help others, I encourage you to use it, no matter what the gift is, and no matter what anyone else says about it.

From all my research of NDEs, experiencing over 2,500 mediumship sessions, and reading over two-hundred different "spiritual" books, I can strongly encourage you to drop any fear of "death." At the same time, please know that your loved ones who have already passed away are in a state of eternal unconditionally loving bliss. Not only does "death" not exist, when we "die," all we do is go "Home." Our perception returns to a reality we agreed to forget about when we incarnated here. We return Home to spirit form, which is actually who we truly are. We are not bodies; we are eternal spirit/energy experiencing life in a borrowed vehicle (the physical body), that will one day cease to exist. (Ecclesiastes 12:7). But *you* never die. The part of you (soul) that is connected to "God" or the "Greater Whole" is eternal.

If you would like to connect with a loved one who has passed away, please know they can hear your prayers and they are still with you. They have not died, and their energy is always with you. You can significantly impact your loved one's energy in spirit just by talking to them or about them, including them in your daily activities, hanging up their picture, or even just thinking about them in a loving way. Spirit has told me over and over that when it is our time to go "Home," it is our time to go. There are no accidents. My father, and your loved ones who have passed away, are supposed to be in a different "mansion" that exists outside our current reality at this very moment.

I want to end this chapter by sharing something with you spirit told me a few years ago. It has stuck with me ever since and I firmly believe it to be absolute truth. I was informed by spirit that the only thing we get to keep when we leave this world is the love we have given and the love we have received. We must leave everything else behind. *In what ways are you giving and receiving love throughout your daily experiences?*

CHAPTER 10

HOW DOES SPIRIT COMMUNICATE?

To answer the question, "How does spirit communicate?" you first must start thinking outside of the limited human mind. You might imagine how hard that is for someone like me who is a reasonable, logical, pragmatic thinker. As I mentioned earlier, when I was sitting next to Deirdre in that restaurant in Boston, when her husband decided to use me as a medium to connect with his wife, I could not understand it. I want to share with you what I have learned over the last four or so years that I have been communicating with the spirit world.

If I must put it in the simplest terms, spirit communication is like a game of charades. When we think outside the limited human mind and languages, we can understand that, as energy, we are eternal. Yes, that means we have always existed, and we will always exist. The concept of creation is a man-made term or understanding. In my opinion – and I know this will ruffle some religious feathers – we were never "created." We have always *been* and always will *be*. It is completely against human logic, and it is impossible to fully understand this concept, but I firmly believe it to be so. The sooner you think outside the mind, the easier it is to understand how communication with spirit actually works.

Since you now can start to try to understand that we are eternal beings as souls and that we are eternally connected to the

Whole, you can start to understand that the soul that was connected to a specific human body here on Earth, still exists. When a medium is connecting with the soul of a person who is not in a human body, that soul is still very much alive. In fact, most people who experience NDEs say they felt more alive when they were "dead" than they ever did while they were "alive." Think about that for a minute. Understanding this concept is essential to spirit communication. I often must remind myself of eternal life during mediumship sessions because spirit communication is so subtle, and it is often difficult to understand with the logical human mind.

So now that you know during a mediumship session, the medium is connecting with an eternal soul who was at one point in-dwelling inside a human body, and with a soul who can be available to communicate, you can now start to better understand the mode of spirit communication. You must remember, as human beings, we operate at a different vibration, and we experience "life" in a different reality than does the soul the medium is connecting with in the spirit world. The departed soul's reality is now in the spirit world, which I believe is our true Home. I don't think we can even come close to understanding what "reality" is like until we return Home to spirit. From what I understand, while in spirit form, we can literally do, create, or experience anything. In spirit, we can be anywhere, at any time, and we are consistently in a state of bliss and love.

Spirit communication does not work at all like the way we as human beings communicate. Spirit uses symbols, feelings, music, analogies, and groups of sounds or letters. Spirit will most often work with the information that is in the medium's human mind. In other words, if I am having a session with a client, and the soul or spirit I'm communicating with wants to communicate with or through a song I have never heard of, the spirit will most likely have to try another song or try something different to get their message to the sitter. I will give some examples later in the book, but for now just be flexible with your understanding as to how spirit communicates with us.

Here, I am going to take you through what a normal mediumship session looks like for me. This outline of a session can change depending on what the spirit wants to share with the sitter. Remember we can all connect with "spirit." In my opinion, God, the Holy Spirit, spirit, our loved ones in spirit, angels, and spirit guides, are all words we use to describe "the other side," and although they may seem to differ from our human perspective or ego mind, I firmly believe that each "energy" is an individual part of the same eternal Whole of Love. I know this seems paradoxical, and I believe it is. We are different, but we are all the same.

Anytime you receive a message to pass on to any human being, or if you receive a message for yourself from "spirit," or "God," you, by definition, are a medium. You don't need someone who says they are a "psychic medium" to connect with the spirit world. As well, communication with spirit is not dangerous if your intentions are pure and you protect yourself with prayers and love.

Before every single mediumship session, I always preface the appointment with at least five minutes of solo meditation and prayer. I ask God for protection, and I ask for Him to shine His Golden White Light over me and my client(s). I ask for the highest good for all parties, including myself. I ask my spirit guides and any available angels for help and support throughout the session. I ask every one of my clients three questions (yes or no answers only):

1. Have you ever been to a medium before?

2. Are you looking to connect with someone specific?

3. If you are looking to connect with someone specific, has the desired person come through in a prior mediumship session?

Those three simple questions occur in the beginning of every mediumship session I perform, as they give me an idea of how the session is going to go. If the answer is "yes" to all three of those questions, I will then remind the client to not focus specifically on the one person they want to connect with because it can significantly interfere with the session. *How?* The spirits that need to come through will come through. The information that needs to be disseminated, will be distributed at the proper time. There is often a difference between what the client is looking for from a mediumship session, and what the spirit world knows can benefit the sitter. The more open-minded the sitter is, and the more flexible they are with what spirit must share with them, the better the session goes. This is part of the reason why I tell people not to book a psychic or mediumship session if they want specific advice on relationships, career, or life choices. Spirit will talk about what spirit knows the person *needs* to know, not what the sitter *wants* to know. Not only that, if you want to consult a psychic/medium to get information on your own personal life path, please try God (or your higher self/soul) for that information. Don't try to obtain specific answers from a "psychic." You are more than capable of obtaining guidance from spirit yourself via prayer.

My job is to help heal the grieving, restore, or increase faith in "God," and remind you that eternal life exists. Other than that, all you need is a little faith, some prayer, and an acknowledgement that there is something bigger than you can currently comprehend.

All answers are within you. You do *not* need to look anywhere outside yourself unless the Universe is guiding you to do so. Trusting that guidance is the key to eternal bliss.

Once the three questions are asked and answered, I pray and meditate again, this time with the sitter. I pray a similar prayer to the one I did prior to the session. In my opinion, this protection and prayer is essential to experience a successful and safe mediumship session.

After the prayer and meditation, we are ready to start our communication with the spirit world. I say "our" communication because the sitter often participates to some degree in a mediumship session. There are times when a medium may not be able to figure out exactly what the spirit is trying to communicate to their loved one still here on Earth.

Other reasons I do this work are because when people grieve the passing of a loved one, they sometimes lose their faith, they can have difficulty functioning in the world, and they often lose their spark for life. I practice mediumship to help people with that. Please remember that spirit communication has nothing to do with the medium besides that this (the medium), is the means by which "God" or "Spirit" communicates with the living. If you currently practice any type of "psychic" or healing work, please humble yourself and realize that it is not you who is providing the healing. The glory goes to "God" or "Source."

There is no better feeling than receiving a message from a client who states that their life has improved exponentially after a session with me. I've received hundreds of messages from clients where the client states that after their mediumship session, they have significantly more faith in God and/or a new spark for life. You can read some of the reviews left by clients on my website at: https://www.danieljohnmedium.com/testimonials. I give credit to Spirit/God for all these reviews.

As we begin our mediumship session, I start to receive what I call "impressions." As I mentioned in Chapter 2, I can only describe these impressions as thoughts in my head. Remember, I do not see spirit with my physical eyes, and I don't hear them with my physical ears. The best way to describe it is that I just "feel" them. Spirit will impress feelings in my mind which I must decipher, and then I relay the proper message to the client.

I often tell clients that in the beginning of a session, it's kind of like a roll call. Spirits will then, often independently, let the sitter know they are "there" by taking turns giving messages. I also tell my clients that as much as they want to connect with a specific person, the message itself is significantly more important than who the message is from. That being said, between the message itself and the feeling the sitter gets, we pretty much know from whom, specifically, the message is from.

Every medium has their own style and their own unique way of communicating with spirit. Some mediums are better at determining male or female energy, while some mediums are better able to receive a detailed description of what the person in spirit looked like when they were "in" a physical body here on Earth. Some mediums will obtain how the spirit passed, and some mediums receive a combination of different things. For some reason, I commonly receive and relay names or groups of letters that will refer to a name I need to discuss, whether it be of a person in spirit or of a person here on Earth. Remember, I know nothing, and do not want to know *anything* about my client before and during a session. I receive song titles, song lyrics, analogies, or one of my many symbols that I mentioned earlier, but I can also pick up on the personality of the spirit while they were incarnate here on Earth as well.

Most often, I will start the session by sharing what I am receiving with my client, which usually includes names, numbers, and a few random things. Those random things can be absolutely anything from "broccoli" to "Tic Tacs.®" It is important to remember that the names I receive, can, again, be those of someone living or in spirit. Many people get confused by this and search for names of people who have passed away. I would say that approximately 70% of the time, the spirit will impress me with the name of a living person with whom they want to communicate to or provide information about. If I am channeling a husband who has passed, the name I receive may be that of the sitter's living child, followed up with a message to or about that specific child. I could receive the name, "Harry," or "Hazel," but the name might actually be, "Hannah," or "Hank." It is not as concrete as I wish it was. The name or names a spirit references will not usually be as far removed as something like "your friend's, father's, brother's nephew's, cousin's former roommate." The names I receive are most often very close and very meaningful to the sitter. Once we figure out the name and who it is about, more information starts to flow.

With numbers, it can, and often does get pretty wild. If I receive the number "27," for whatever reason, it can mean so many things. It can be an age, a date of the month, or even someone's sports jersey number. It can be an address, a lucky number, or even February 7, like 2/7. I once had a session where I kept receiving the number "53." We tried everything and could not figure it out.

I finally asked, "Was someone 5'3"?"

My client laughed and said, "Ugggh, my ex-husband, but he is still alive."

I said, "Really, he is exactly 5'3"?"

She said, "That is what it says on his driver's license."

As soon as she said that, even though he is still alive, I got an immediate impression that there was a significant forgiveness opportunity that spirit wanted her to address. We continued on this one topic for about fifteen minutes as she received a plethora of validating information to help her on her forgiveness journey with her ex.

I have had experiences with numbers that would blow your mind. On one occasion, while I was providing an online group mediumship session, I was connecting a father with his son in spirit. I said the number "24," and the father immediately started getting emotional. He then lifted his arm up so the camera could display that he had that exact number tattooed on him in honor of his late son. His son then proceeded to give his father many beautiful messages of faith, healing, and hope from "the other side."

Once we determine which spirit wants to communicate with us, and what they generally want to "talk" about, things start to get very interesting. In some sessions, the details can be vague, but meaningful, hard to figure out, and a bit choppy. More often however, sessions include very strong, very specific, extremely powerful, and undeniable validations.

The overall quality of a session varies significantly. This polarity is often due to one or more of the following factors:

• My energy

- My client's energy

- God's plan

- Spirit

- Sitter error

- Medium error

- The cosmos (full moon, planetary transits, etc.)

- Fear

- Anxiety

- Degree of grief

- Skepticism

- Lack of being open-minded

There are many other factors that can contribute to a session's overall quality. However, 99% of the mediumship sessions I have had the blessing of facilitating, are powerful, healing, full of love, and more than anything else, they restore faith in "God," and/or bring forth clarity regarding a higher purpose to the client's life.

Most sessions can range from one to two hours. I only offer one-hour sessions on my website, but if spirit wants the session to go longer, I always honor it. My clients never incur any additional charges if the session goes over an hour. I had a session recently that went over two hours. Not a dime more was collected, and the sitter was very thankful for the session and for the extra time.

The amount of love, healing, faith, and mind-blowing, detailed information that a mediumship session provides is beyond explanation. Later in the book I will share five stories that will give you an abundance of goosebumps. Each story is beautiful and illustrates that God's Love/plan is greater than we can even imagine.

In a mediumship session, once I receive an impression, there is almost always a message behind it. Spirit usually mentions three things in order of probability of occurrence:

1. Something that the sitter recently experienced

2. Something that happened right before or after the deceased loved one passed

3. A story or special memory that was shared throughout the sitter's time with the spirit while they were together on Earth

I had a session recently where I was connecting a young woman to her mother and grandmother in the spirit world. They "showed" me (made me think of) the fruit candy, Mamba®. Sure enough, the sitter had bought Mamba® Fruit Chews just the other day, and she was eating them at work the day of her session. It was a simple, "I am with you," from her mom on the other side. If I would have simply said, "Your mom is with you," that would not have been as meaningful if it wasn't backed up with something that the client snacked on literally hours before the session. And it wasn't an apple or something more common, it was Mamba® Fruit Chews of all things!

More often than not, when I get an impression, whether it's a symbol, or an actual thing, like a specific item, song, or any other details, it's the message that accompanies the evidential item that means more than the item itself. For instance, take the Mamba® candy that was mentioned in the previous example. The message was not about the Mamba® Fruit Chews specifically. In that case, the mother in spirit mentioned something very specific that her daughter recently experienced to let her know that her mom is always/still with her. There is so much depth to spirit communication.

In another example, I experienced a mediumship session with a woman named Marcy, whose son, Gregor, transitioned Home at just four-years old. During the session, I received an impression of someone jumping off a building with a parachute. Little did I know that Marcy's son was, unfortunately, pushed off a bridge to his death. This visual impression Gregor shared with me helped his mother understand that he is at peace, and he did not feel any pain she may have assumed he felt or experienced from his fall. I also explained to her that even though his passing was tragic, he had a significant amount of support from the "other side" as he transitioned back Home to spirit. This visual was also validation that it really was Marcy's son in spirit connecting with her through me. There is no way I could have known his cause of death or what he wanted to share with his mother. That information came from Gregor's soul and was given to his mother via his medium of choice. Can you see the power, beauty, love, and peace that comes from one simple message like that? It is absolutely beautiful!

Throughout a mediumship session there are often anywhere from twenty to thirty messages for the sitter. Some sessions have a few less and some have a few more. Most sessions have at least one specific person come through and some have had up to ten spirits show up. Some sessions are more counseling and less mediumship, but whatever comes through is *always* what is best for the sitter. Neither the sitter nor I will know how the session may go.

I once had a session with a woman, and her grandmother came through immediately. After Grandma was done, my mind went blank. I even had to step outside so I could try to figure out what was going on. As I walked back into the session, I felt spirit guide me to open my mind as to what my client needed, which was possibly outside of communicating with a specific family member in spirit. As I walked back into my office, I was compelled to ask her if she experienced an extreme trauma during her childhood. Sure enough, she broke into tears and the healing started.

After well over an hour, we both realized that it wasn't communication with a specific soul who passed away that my client needed, it was more of a counseling session about some previous trauma she experienced earlier in her life. We both honored spirit because God knew what she needed more than we both did. It ended up being an extremely healing session. Spirit even provided me with the name of a book I should recommend to her. I had never heard of the book, but we looked it up, and not only was it an actual book, but the sitter messaged me weeks later to tell me that she completed reading the book, and it was exactly what she needed to read at that particular time in her life. The Holy Spirit/spirit is *so* powerful.

No matter how a session plays out, there is always healing and an abundance of love that both the sitter and I get to experience. At the conclusion of any session, I always offer the sitter the opportunity to ask questions. Upon completion of a mediumship session, it is imperative to pray as well as ask for protection and removal of any residual energy that may have attached itself to me or my client. I usually do a little hand wave and I picture myself engulfed in God's White Light of Infinite Unconditional Love. Sometimes I stand under a light bulb, close my eyes, and take a "God shower." I thank God for this gift of mediumship, pray for extra protection, and release everyone and everything to its highest good. I then go about the rest of my day.

As mentioned earlier, I e-mail every single client a recording of their session within twenty-four hours. I often get e-mails from clients after their session, where they share with me things they couldn't validate during the appointment. In a typical session, approximately 80% to 85% of the information from spirit is validated during the session. From my experience, 5% to 10% of the remaining information that was passed on during a session is validated within the next year, leaving 5% to 10% to most likely never be validated.

The healing and number of layers that are involved in a mediumship session are truly beyond understanding. As you will see in the amazing stories shared at the end of this book, the power of the spirit world is undeniable and there are no coincidences or accidents. Everything is in perfect Divine order.

CHAPTER 11

YOU (YES, *YOU*) ARE A MEDIUM

Another definition of "medium" according to *Merriam-Webster Dictionary* is: "A particular form or system of communication (such as newspapers, radio, or television)." Therefore, when you communicate with a loved one – or any spirit for that matter – in the nonphysical world/realm, and you pass that information on to another person, you, by definition, are a medium.

Anyone can be a medium between the spirit world and the physical world. Have you ever been guided to tell someone something (given them advice or relayed a message of some sort), and you don't know how you obtained the information? The Holy Spirit, or "God," or a passed loved one, was able to impress information onto or into your mind so you were able to help another human being. There is no separation in the spirit world. We are all one universal "Ocean of Love." It is one big paradox. We are all One and we are each an individual part of that Whole, but we are all still connected as One Love. Let that one soak in.

In my first book, "Why Are We Here?" I explained how we can live our lives with love. Being kind, having compassion for others, serving "God" (the Greater Whole), smiling, forgiving, and just loving all others is the best way to be. When you do these things, you raise your vibration – your energy – making yourself better equipped to receive messages/guidance from "Spirit" or

"Home." The more you are in alignment with your soul, the better you can communicate with the spirit world.

As a medium, I not only connect with other people's loved ones in spirit, but I also connect with my own loved ones, my spirit guides, and the Holy Spirit/God in general. This spiritual guidance is something that can help you live on your highest path in life. A spirit guide, from what I understand, is a soul (energy) who has agreed to be available to you for some, or all, of your physical life, depending on your soul contract. You can ask for, and receive guidance from, the spirit world any time you desire. (Matthew 7:7). When you realize that you are a soul experiencing "life" as a human being, and you recognize there are "energies" who are always available to you, life becomes a much more enjoyable experience.

My absolute favorite Bible verse is Proverbs 3:5-6. The New International Version (NIV) states Proverbs 3:5-6 as: "Trust in the Lord with all your heart and lean not on your own understanding; in all your ways submit to Him, and He will make your paths straight." I would like to summarize what this verse means to me. If you start thinking with the real part of you – the soul or Love – and you let that Love guide you, as opposed to using ego and fear to make decisions and experience life with, you can experience bliss here on Earth.

I mention in my first book about all the times that I (Daniel), wanted to do X, Y, and Z, but God, or the Universe, or something or someone in spirit, was guiding me a different way. To this day, I listen to spiritual guidance every single time, even if I don't understand or agree with it. For instance, recently, spirit told me to take a two week break from social media. I listened, of course, and as much as I missed it, I could feel how much I needed that break.

Trust, love, and guidance from the spirit world is what contributes to anyone having a blissful life. We all can experience this type of abundance and peace even when life throws us some extreme difficulties, sadness, or grief. The spirit world often knows what is better for our lives than we do. Please be open to guidance from spirit because your life will never be the same once you trust there is a team on "the other side" ready, willing, and able to help you.

When it comes to communicating with my own loved ones in spirit, it can be quite difficult figuring out what they are trying to share with me. As I mentioned earlier, the less I know about the sitter before and during a session, the better the session is. Therefore, when I am connecting with one of my own loved ones, whether the information is intended for me, a family member, or for a friend, it is significantly more difficult to determine the message. So, it is very common for many grieving people not to realize when their own loved ones are communicating with them. Let me share with you how you can connect with your own loved ones in spirit.

As I mentioned just once or twice already, you do not need someone who claims to be a "psychic medium" to communicate with your loved ones who have passed away. I do what I do as a medium because all too often, people simply don't understand the ins and outs of spirit communication. Grief is a big blocker of a strong connection with the spirit world, so please go easy on yourself when you experience loss, and you feel that a person who has passed away is not communicating with you.

In the following paragraphs I will guide on how you can connect with your loved ones in spirit without another "medium" besides yourself. The process of aligning yourself to communicate with the spirit world, and your own loved ones, takes time. Practice these things daily and often, to better accommodate your spiritual communications:

First and most importantly, I ask you to pray. This has nothing to do with any specific religion or ritual. When I say pray, I mean that you simply have a positive thought with a desired intention. I encourage you to acknowledge that you are part of something bigger that you cannot fully comprehend. Understand that the false you (the ego), doesn't know all the answers, and at your core, you are simply love. Ask whomever or whatever you want, that is an energy in spirit, for support, protection, and unconditional love. This first step is vital to align the human you to the real you (your soul). This alignment is like tuning an old-school radio tuner to the correct frequency. When you adjust the dial on an antique radio to the correct megahertz, the signal can become very strong and very clear. This is exactly what you are doing in this first step. You are putting yourself at the vibrational frequency needed to connect with the spirit world. Pray for guidance with this.

The next thing you can do to ensure you are able to connect to the spirit world is to simply love. As I mentioned earlier in the chapter, earlier in this book, and many times in my first book, love will lead to downright abundance and bliss. What does "love" include? I would say the answer to this is subjective, but I would also say that we all inherently know what true love is. After praying, being loving is essential to proper and effective spirit communication for others and for yourself. Be kind to others, have compassion, forgive others, and forgive yourself. Make ethical decisions, treat others how you want to be treated, and recognize that you are an eternal soul living life in a human body.

Recognize that no matter what shows up in your "reality," it is up to you how to react to it. All too often, we, as human beings, lead with ego, anger, fear, jealousy, hatred, and lust, among other things. I feel these are what many people call, "sin," "satan," "demons," or the "devil." These are words used to describe fear/ego-based decisions instead of love-based decisions. The more we choose love over fear, we raise our vibration, which gets us more "in tune" with the spirit world. Once you pray and choose love over fear daily, you are on to the easier practices that will better enable you to let spirit guide you to your highest path. Then you are better equipped to serve others and yourself.

Practicing meditation is an amazing way to better facilitate communication with spirit. Meditation has been clinically proven to help with patience, sleep, anxiety, disease, as well as providing many other benefits. I wrote a short chapter on meditation in my previous book, but there are many books and media available on how to meditate. Prayer, love, and meditation are easily the top three things that will enable you to be better guided by spirit. Practicing these three simple things daily for the rest of your life can provide a consistently amazing experience for you regardless of what shows up in your "reality."

I created, and currently teach, a three-level course called "Understanding Energy and Mediumship Development." In these classes, I teach my students the proper way to understand who we are as human beings and how to work with energy (our real self). I also share my experiences with mediumship, so my students are better equipped to help the grieving who seek them out.

I teach my students that trust is the most important thing you need after the three core essentials listed previously (prayer, love, and meditation). Without trust, spirit communication is simply not possible. All mediums – you included – connect with the spirit world differently. It is common, however, that spirit communication is subtle, not concrete, and not black and white. Therefore, the more you trust whatever you are sensing, feeling, hearing, seeing, tasting, or smelling – even if it is not with your five senses, which is most often the case – the better you will be able to accurately understand what spirit is trying to communicate to you. Since spirit communication can be extremely subtle, trust is the ultimate hurdle when trying to interpret messages from the spirit world.

Up to this point, I have shared that meditation, prayer, being a loving person, and trust, are essential foundations in order to be better able to communicate with spirit. Once you nail those down, the rest is easy. What helped me understand mediumship more was reading books authored by mediums, so I could better understand how each author facilitated their own communication with spirit. At the beginning of my mediumship journey, I read over fifty books in about eighteen months, many of which were written by mediums. I absorbed a plethora of information and I learned so much by reading these books. I came to understand that although spirit communication worked differently for each medium, there were many commonalities among them. Some mediums can literally see spirit with their physical eyes. I am kind of glad I don't. Some mediums get names, while others don't get names at all. Some mediums are able to describe how a soul/person looked while they were here in the physical, and some mediums can sense male or female energy while others are not able to do so. It is very interesting to see how other mediums work. I encourage you to seek out books written by mediums so you can better understand how spirit communication works for each of them.

Some of the most common signs and symbols spirit uses to communicate with us are as follows:

• Animals/birds/insects. Your loved one will often use the energy of a particular animal or insect as a way to get your attention and to get a message to you. Remember, your loved one is not the actual animal or insect.

• Songs/music. These musical impressions can come in the form of a favorite song heard on the radio, or a medium may receive a song title, song lyrics, or the name of a band that has a significant amount of meaning for the spirit and/or the sitter.

• Analogies. These are often very complicated, but they are also very exciting, and are most often wonderful experiences. The spirit will often find many different ways to compare something here in the physical world with the information they want to relay from the other side. There are many layers involved with these types of validations.

• Symbols. Many mediums will receive a symbol which has their own unique meaning behind it. In this way, the spirit can easily pass on a message to conserve the medium's energy. I have given you some examples of my symbols throughout the book.

• Signs/synchronistic experiences. Whether you are driving in your vehicle or you are in your own home, these synchronistic experiences can be overwhelming, powerful, multi-layered, and full of love.

• Random thoughts. When you think of your loved one, it may not be as random as one might think. When you are thinking of a lost loved one, it is often their energy directly communicating with you at that very moment. Pay attention to your thoughts and keep them positive.

• Numbers. These beautiful experiences can be found as times on the clock, on license plates, on receipts, or as numbers on a ticket, for example. Seeing repeating numbers, number sequences, and/or numbers that correspond to a specific date or specific time is extremely common. Pay attention and trust.

I always tell people not to "stretch it." Many times, you can make things fit if you really want them to. That is why it is so important to trust, be patient, and know that spirit communication will occur at the exact moment and location that the Universe wants you to experience it. Please don't force it. Pray, meditate, love unconditionally, and trust what spirit wants to share with you. God/The Universe doesn't mess up, and everything happens on His/Her/Its' time, not ours.

CHAPTER 12

REACHING OUT TO A PSYCHIC/MEDIUM FOR GUIDANCE

As a medium, part of my job is to help people better understand and navigate grief, increase their faith in God and/or the afterlife, help people connect with their loved ones in spirit, help people live their best lives possible, and spread God's unconditional love.

During some mediumship sessions, spirit will guide me to pass on information to the sitter, or receiver, that has nothing to do with a specific deceased loved one. In fact, there are many times when very validating life-changing information will come through for a sitter without knowing who specifically the information is coming from. The Holy Spirit can use me to help guide the sitter with anything from career and relationship advice to tips on how to forgive themselves or others.

However, the reason I only offer "mediumship sessions" is because that is what spirit has guided me to do. Therefore, I do not offer "psychic readings" or "fortune telling." I have met many people in the spiritual community who do offer these types of services. I have nothing against this work, but I choose to focus on mediumship and pass on whatever spirit feels is best for the sitter. I do not want people coming to me for specific answers to questions they have about any situation in their lives. In my opinion, these types of answers are attainable via prayer, not by consistently seeking out a "medium" or a "psychic."

I feel when we are at the right vibration or energy, we are self-sufficient, and we are fully capable of receiving personal guidance from spirit. However, when we grieve, for instance, we are limited from our natural ability to receive guidance from "Home," or the spirit world. We are also restricted from spiritual guidance when we do things that lower our vibration, such as drink alcohol, gamble, lie, cheat, steal, or fear. Therefore, God will use people like mediums, clergy, counselors, or even strangers to help and/or guide others in life with whatever gifts the medium may be endowed with.

If you would like to reach out to a psychic or medium, all I ask is that you pray first and perform a self-evaluation. *Why are you seeking this guidance externally? What can you do to raise your vibration?* (Please refer to my first book for tips on how to raise your vibration). *Are you truly in need of someone else – a medium, for instance – to connect to spirit for you because of grief and/or other limiting factors?* If so, pray, and let the Universe guide you. If not, see if you are able to receive guidance from God/Spirit without having to seek His support through someone else. We are all connected to "The Universe," or "Source," or "God." You are part of It. (Psalms 82). "It" is in you (Romans 5:5) (2 Corinthians 1:22), and since you are part of "It," you can obtain information and receive guidance from "It" without looking anywhere else but within you, which is part of "It." "Listen to your heart, it knows all things because it came from the Soul of the World, and it will one day return there." (*The Alchemist,* Paulo Coelho.)

Again, I do what I do because grief is a severe block for connection to Source. For instance, some parents whose children transition before they do, often can't find the strength to get back to living after their child passes away. I have performed well over 1,000 mediumship sessions for parents who have suffered the physical loss of one or more of their children. The amount of healing, love, understanding, increased faith in God, and resurgence of a spark for life that comes as a result of these sessions is absolutely breathtaking. I have had parents tell me that one session with a medium has done more for them than years of therapy did. If you are severely grieving, I truly feel a session with a medium can be life-changing for you. If you are not grieving from the loss of a loved one or suffering from some other major traumatic life experience, but you are just looking for some specific guidance, please seek God first before you pay someone to access this information for you. You are more than capable of obtaining guidance from spirit any time you wish. I learned this lesson the hard way.

I would like to share a personal story with you. This is hard for me to write, but it is something that taught me a major lesson in life. The reason I am sharing this with you is to help you understand the danger of depending on others – psychics or mediums for instance – for spiritual guidance or relying on anything but God's direct guidance for you when navigating your life.

Early in 2021, my wife and I went through a very difficult time in our marriage. With three kids and with both of us being very busy with work and other activities, after eleven years of marriage, we hit a wall. As our relationship started to fail, I found myself looking for guidance from psychics and other mediums because I felt like I was getting mixed messages when I prayed about it.

Please remember that because I keep myself at a high vibration with prayer, gratitude, forgiveness, and constant love, among other things, I am more than capable of receiving guidance directly from Source without having to seek elsewhere. What I did is what I am telling you not to do. I was not grieving, and I was in a very good place (other than with the marriage thing), and I proactively sought guidance from others without listening to His guidance (which I could not understand at the time). And boy, did God ever teach me a lesson, so I can teach you a lesson.

As I continued to pray and receive mixed signals from Spirit/God on whether my wife and I were supposed to stay together or not, I reached out to a "psychic" friend of mine. I asked her if my wife and I were going to get divorced soon and she immediately told me, "Yes." She went on to say that we were not soul mates and she felt that when she first met us. She continued by saying that she knew it would soon be time for us to separate. I was devastated, to say the least. I pretended she never said that and thought maybe she could be wrong. I reached out to another "psychic" friend, and she pretty much told me the same exact thing.

As our marriage continued to deteriorate, I started getting to the point of acceptance of this "psychic determined" fate. One day while on TikTok, I came across a video of a woman who was answering questions from the viewers. There were over four-hundred people on this video and when I wrote, "Is it time to move on?" in the chat, this "psychic" immediately responded with an overwhelming, "Yes, it's time to move on." My wife came home about ten minutes later and my energy from that video chat enabled us to get into one of our biggest fights ever. At this point, I was determined that it was our time to move on and go our own separate ways.

As our marriage continued to get progressively worse, I thought I would reach out to one more "psychic medium" friend of mine to determine my fate. Again, remember, other than my wife and I not getting along at all, I was operating at a very high vibration, serving God, helping others, and performing high-quality mediumship sessions. This enabled me to be more than capable of receiving guidance from God without needing to proactively seek out guidance from others. I should have simply prayed and trusted what God was telling me – which was to stay and work it out, even though it seemed hopeless. However, if I had done that, you would not be reading this, but since you are, you may now be less likely to make the same mistake I did. *You're welcome.* This last attempt to get information from a "psychic" resulted in the same determination as all three other requests did. This "psychic" said our marriage was over, and she informed me that we would be divorced before the end of 2021. I had convinced myself that all these "psychics" and "mediums" were right, and divorce was inevitable.

I continued praying, even though four "psychics" said our relationship was over. I asked God if there was any way to work this out because I did not want to get divorced. It was a completely out-of-the-blue text I received from a man whom I had never met, that would help me understand that God had a much bigger role in my life than any "medium" or "psychic" did. Not so coincidentally, this text from someone I had only connected with recently and virtually, and who knew nothing whatsoever about my marital situation, came at an extremely pivotal time.

A man named Brock messaged me at a very low point in my marriage. He texted me, out of the blue, at a time when I thought it was inevitable that my wife and I would be getting divorced very soon. He sent me a sermon about marriage and God's intention for it. Thing is, there is no way he could have known about our difficulties without a pure connection with the Divine/Holy Spirit himself. This not so random text from Brock motivated me to pray more about the whole situation with my wife and to try not to listen to what others had to say when I *proactively* asked them about divorce.

I felt that when I let God lead the way and I trusted in His guidance as opposed to trying to find answers elsewhere, things went a lot smoother. My wife and I ended up working things out and our relationship is now better than it has ever been.

All I ask of you is that you pray to whatever Higher Source you believe in and trust what you feel when you get guidance from "It." Don't depend on any "psychic" or "medium" to answer questions about your life. Proverbs 3:5-6 is a great verse to refer to. All answers are within you, and God will give them to you when He knows you need them, not when you think you need them. Those are two very different things.

It may seem odd that a medium is telling you not to seek anyone outside yourself for answers, but please pay attention to what I am saying. God will use all His people to help others when He knows they need guidance. We, as humans, are extremely limited with our human way of thinking. Trust in Source/Spirit and pray about things first. Then, with guidance from the spirit world, you can follow your heart – the love part of you/your soul. If what you receive involves having an appointment with a medium, then trust that.

Again, please remember that grief often blocks connection with the spirit world, so go easy on yourself. People often ask me how one can tell the difference between what their spirit-guided heart is telling them to do and what the ego or human brain is telling them to do. The answer is simple: When you take your own personal gain, fear, and ego out of the equation, the answers become crystal clear. When you do things based in love (soul), you raise your vibration, thereby allowing guidance from spirit to be simple and obvious. Let the Universe show you your best path. Trust it, and then take it. It all comes down to trust.

CHAPTER 13

WHAT TO EXPECT FROM A SESSION WITH A MEDIUM

Whether you have visited a medium previously or not, there are many things to consider before you even think about making an appointment. There are also many things you can do to prepare for a session with a medium that will make your time together more effective. I firmly believe in Divine timing, so please remember that God's timing can be, and often is, significantly different from our timing. Spirit is always right because as humans, we think, act with, and are distorted by, our ego. So, when and if, God wants you to sit down with a medium, you will know it, and it will happen. Trust!

Before you even begin the search to find a medium to book a session with, all I ask you to do is to pray first. It doesn't matter what religion you are, or even if you are an atheist, prayer (a thought with a positive intention/affirmation), will guide you in the right direction. There is something greater than us, and you can choose to call that something "God," or whatever you feel inspired to call It.

When we grieve, we go through many stages. First is denial, then anger, then bargaining, then depression, and finally, acceptance. You don't have to be at a certain stage of grief to visit a medium, but I feel that most often, the further along you are in the grief process, the better. As you will read later in this book however, I had a woman book a session with me eight months in advance, and she then passed away the same exact day of her scheduled session. The evening she passed, this woman came through from the other side with so much love and validation for her family that I had to share the story with you in this book. (Chapter 17). It was an amazingly healing session for their entire family even though it was less than twenty-four hours after the matriarch of their family suddenly passed away. Just trust that when the time for you to visit a medium is right, you will know, and it will simply happen.

When the time comes for you to book a session with a medium, there are a few important things to consider when deciding on which medium you end up moving forward with. I feel strongly that if you ask for guidance from spirit as to which medium would best fit you and your energy, you will receive direction from The Universe. Here are a few important things to remember when selecting the medium who is right for you:

After praying for guidance regarding this, please pay attention to signs and feelings as you go through the discovery/booking process. Maybe a post from a specific medium continues to show up on your social media feed. Maybe you run into a friend who shares with you that they just had an amazing experience with a medium. Remember, that spirit communication can be extremely subtle, but is often very powerful. If you ask, you will receive. I cannot tell you how many times I have had a session with someone, and at the end they tell me something along the lines of, "You will not believe how I found you!"

As you are guided to a specific medium, it is very important to check their website. If they don't have one, that is the first red flag. Once you have confirmed the medium has a legitimate website, I highly recommend checking out their social media sites. Look for reviews and read them all. In my opinion, if they do not have reviews, that is another red flag. Any honest and legitimate medium will have reviews on their website and/or social media pages. As you look at their website, evaluate how you feel, and pay attention to the energy you sense while viewing all their platforms. Check their pricing. If the medium's services are too expensive or too inexpensive, these can be red flags as well. Even though pricing is very subjective, there seems to be a fair price to pay for these kinds of services. Most genuine mediums who are offering respectable services offer very reasonable prices. One-hour sessions should range from $100 for new mediums without much of a track record and few reviews, to $300 per hour for well-known respected mediums with many great reviews. If prices are outside of this range, you should seriously consider the medium's motives and/or possible quality of their services. Like anything else in this world, services are not free. Mediumship sessions take time, effort, preparation, and most of all, energy. You would not believe how much energy it takes to do this work.

Be sure to confirm on the medium's website, or when you book the appointment, that the medium you are meeting with either lets you record the session, or the medium records the session and sends it to you after the appointment. If it is not stated, ask the medium if it is okay to record the session yourself. If the answer is "no" to getting a recording of the session, that's another red flag. I have recorded every session and sent the recording to every single one of my clients because I feel that it is very important for the client to have the session available for review later. There are many things that are not validated during mediumship sessions because most sitters are nervous and/or severely grieving, therefore they don't get the full experience until they listen back to the recording.

One more thing to consider before you book an appointment with a medium is if you truly feel ready to do so. There are times when we grieve so hard that even though we may think we are ready, we are not. How can you tell if you are ready to see a medium? I would say the answer to that question is that you have absolute trust in the medium you chose, and you are not determined to get any specific information that you desire, as opposed to the information spirit knows you need. There is no timetable to determine if you are ready or not. Everyone grieves at their own pace, so please try to make an honest assessment of your grief and your energy before you book a mediumship session.

Once your appointment is booked, it is time to get excited. Some mediums are booked out a few weeks while some are booked out for years, believe it or not. Plan accordingly, and be prepared for your session. *How do you get prepared?* It is the simplest answer: Opening your heart and mind is the most important thing. Do not have any expectations and let spirit run the session. Don't over-analyze, don't overthink, and most of all, relax and trust the process. Let spirit, through the medium, do their work.

Since I am a skeptic by nature, and I am an analytical thinker, when I went to my first appointment with a medium, I was not a good sitter. I was not as open as I should have been. I wanted to connect with my dad, and him alone, and I wanted him to say very specific things. That is *not* how the session went at all. However, my dad did come through, along with many other loved ones. I have listened to that recording over thirty times in the last four years. I still learn something new every single time I listen to it.

Open your heart, open your mind, and make sure you are able to receive a recording of your session before you book. Don't forget!

In my opinion, it is very important to pray daily, in general, but I feel it is extremely beneficial to do so the entire week before your mediumship appointment. I feel it is also very helpful to meditate the week before as well. Prayer and meditation will align your energy to receive whatever information spirit would like to relay to you. I want to mention here, again, that you do not need to go to a medium to connect to spirit or with your loved ones specifically. In my opinion, we are all "mediums," as I believe each and every one of us can connect to, as well as receive and relay messages from the spirit world.

The reason I do what I do is because people can be stuck in a state of severe grief, virtually eliminating the possibility of obtaining information from God/Spirit/their soul/ themselves. In order to connect to the spirit world, it is highly recommended that your energy is at a high vibration. *What does this mean?* I might have said this a few times already in this book, but I will repeat it, so it sinks in. Your energetic vibration rises when you focus on love. You can raise your vibration by being kind, showing compassion, exercising forgiveness, and practicing non-judgment toward others. You operate with love when you realize that everyone in this world is a brother or sister to you regardless of any perceived difference from you. Universal Love does not exclude anyone. Raise your vibration by practicing unconditional love and you can live your dream life. *Why?* Because you understand that you are love at your core and expressing that love to all simply aligns you with who you truly are as spirit/love. There are many people who have incarnated here to demonstrate this Universal Love.

So, the last few minutes before your appointment, you are sitting in your car, or you're by your phone or your computer. You are nervous and excited at the same time. Remember your prayers and meditation. Ask God for His extra protection during this time. Ask your spirit guides and angels to be with you. Take some deep breaths and trust. Open your heart, open your mind, and go for it. Just let it happen. Do not overthink it and release all expectations. Most of all, I want you to trust the process and know you are exactly where you need to be at that very moment.

After the mediumship session is complete, it is common to have some homework to do. There are often names you probably didn't know or recognize at the time of the session, and it is likely there were some details you couldn't figure out. This is okay and is to be expected. After my first session with a medium, it took me months to figure out some of the messages from spirit, but when I did, it was more than amazing. Once the session is finished, thank God for His guidance, and continue on your path at a high vibration so you can serve God by serving others.

As you can tell by now, I firmly believe we all come from something greater. You can call "It" whatever you'd like, but, in my opinion, "It" is all the same thing. Information from that Source is always right, and it's always for your highest good. As I mentioned previously, when we grieve and/or don't vibrate at a high vibration, we often limit ourselves from accessing very useful information from the spirit world. This is why many people, such as mediums, spiritual teachers, clergy and even some "random people," are put in the presence of a grieving person in order to guide them along their path. Jesus is my absolute favorite teacher, medium, and reflection of Light and Love/God.

CHAPTER 14

PIGGYBACKING

I would like to dedicate an entire chapter to this topic because of the overwhelming amount of understanding and healing that can take place when you accept this phenomenon. To understand this concept, again, like other things in this book, it is important to step outside of the logical mind and stray from the "normal" way of thinking.

"Piggybacking" is a term used in the spiritual/mediumship community to explain how souls in the spirit world will "team up" to deliver multiple messages to multiple people simultaneously. This occurs in a group mediumship session when one sitter is directly receiving very specific information, via the medium, such as names, numbers, and specific details, while another attendee is relating to the same specific information with detailed validation for them as well. The logical mind says that the person who is directly receiving a message from spirit through the medium is the only person it is for and from the single soul/person whom it is from. I am here to tell you it is not that black and white at all.

Piggybacking has happened in almost every single in-person and online group mediumship session I have ever hosted. Piggybacking is a little more common with groups of people who are strangers, as opposed to when I visit a person's home or provide an online session where all the sitters know each other.

When I first started practicing mediumship, I began to host live events on Facebook on Monday evenings. These events have anywhere from two hundred to six hundred people watching at one time. During these live virtual events, I bring on multiple sitters, one at a time, throughout the evening. Anywhere from two to five people join me on the live video, individually, with the intention of receiving specific detailed messages from their loved ones in spirit through me, the medium. I am not talking about simple "I love you" and "I miss you" messages. I am talking about very specific, detailed messages, like names, birthdays, and in-depth evidential communication from spirit. After every single virtual or in-person live event, I received up to five e-mails or messages from other attendees who felt that the specific information that was communicated by spirit, directly to another sitter, was for them. I would encourage them to not stretch it to make it fit.

As more and more viewers shared how they specifically related to the details that were expressed and validated by other sitters – which were extremely accurate and specific – I could not comprehend how that could possibly work.

How can I be having a session with one client, while hundreds of other people are watching, but the very specific information provided to the sitter, could be intended for, and at the same time, be validated by other people as well? As I started to experience this phenomenon, I continuously chalked it up to coincidence. I was convinced these other attendees were forcing the messages from spirit to fit their own situations, when the information coming through from spirit was intended for someone else. Then, my perspective changed when I experienced piggybacking first-hand.

In October 2018, about four months after I announced to the world that I am a medium, I attended an event hosted by Theresa Caputo, the "Long Island Medium." As my wife and I sat in a crowd of over 2,000 people, I didn't expect Theresa would give me a "reading." About halfway through the event, she started connecting with a father in spirit who wanted to connect with his son here in the physical world. She chose – or spirit chose – a particular man from the audience. Remember, at this point, I had already started to receive some messages from attendees at my own live events where other people felt the actual direct sitter's mediumship session was either for them as well, or they felt I had the wrong person. I just chalked it up to coincidence every time.

As Theresa started connecting this man with his father in spirit, some of the things she said the spirit was sharing were extremely specific regarding my own father who had passed. Theresa started talking about a wallet and a watch. I have both of those from my dad. *Coincidence, right?* Possibly. Then she said to the man, "I must talk about the number '4' and/or the month of April."

That's weird, I thought. *Dad passed away four years ago this month and I have one sister whose name is April.*

I started to listen more attentively. There was no question it was this man's father connecting with him through Theresa, the medium, *but it was my dad too!* She continued with ten to twelve very specific, accurate messages for this man, that he validated, and was visibly emotional about. I don't understand how, and I don't understand why, but my father piggybacked with this man's father in spirit.

The messages continued to get stronger and more detailed for this man, as well as for me. The "reading" even contained two very specific, not too common sayings that my dad had shared with me at times during his life. I don't remember all the specific messages from Theresa, but it was incredible, and inexplicably healing to me. I wish I would have written them down, but I didn't. My advice to you is to bring a pen and paper to any private or group mediumship session you attend.

Without experiencing piggybacking for myself, I would've never believed the hundreds of people who have messaged me with detailed validation from their loved ones in spirit while I was providing a mediumship session to someone else. I would have continued to attribute these situations to coincidence or randomness if I didn't personally experience piggybacking as the "sitter."

Now, about four years later, after almost every single in-person or online group mediumship event that I host, some observers continuously inform me about how detailed messages that were directly given to another sitter, resonated with them beyond comprehension.

Recently, in a sold-out event, the first woman I gave a direct mediumship session to was sitting next to a woman who had the same birthday, and their mothers had the same first name. They even shared a few other very specific things in common. If that was the first time I had experienced this, I would have said it was just a coincidence. Due to the hundreds of times I have experienced piggybacking, I am not surprised one bit anymore, *Well, I kind of still am.*

Even though piggybacking is a difficult concept to understand, please trust me that it is both powerful and Divine. If you are attending a group mediumship session, pay attention, even if the medium is not directly speaking to you. Don't stretch it to fit, but trust that your loved ones will take any opportunity to communicate with you, even if it is during a mediumship session that is directed at someone else.

CHAPTER 15

THE MODERN DAY ROLE OF MEDIUMSHIP

If there is ever a time to be more connected to the spiritual world, that time is now. In a world full of ego and fear, we as humans can always benefit from guidance and support from spirit. The Earth has often been a host to tragic events like wars, famine, injustice, and hatred. In my opinion, communication with the spirit world is needed now more than ever because we are in the information age. At any moment, a person can pick up their phone and access an abundance of information. Type anything in the search bar on your phone or computer and you will be virtually whisked away to a host of seemingly unlimited information. This information can be peaceful, loving, and beautiful, but unfortunately, someone who does not have the best of intentions can spread significant amounts of fear into this world via the Internet.

Have you noticed that more TV shows like "Long Island Medium" with Theresa Caputo, and "Life after Death" with Tyler Henry are being created for the public? In my opinion, there is an overwhelming request from God for more of us as human beings to believe in something greater than ourselves. You can call "It" whatever you'd like, but "It" has been requesting our attention for a very long time. If we could simply understand that we, as human beings, all come from something greater, we are more connected to

"It" than we can imagine, and He/She loves each and every one of us eternally and unconditionally, the world would become a better place to learn, grow, and love.

In the thousands of mediumship sessions I have performed over the years, the amount of love, healing, increased faith in something greater, and understanding of eternal life that has resulted, is beyond words. I do this work as a medium to let people know that, from what I understand, we do not die. When a parent experiences their child transition before they do, a mediumship session that includes messages from that child, is beyond healing. When some people lose a loved one's physical presence from their experience, it can have a severely detrimental effect on their life. Grief can tear a person away from a belief in "God." Grief can lead to severe depression, substance abuse, and even suicide. After meeting with a medium who can connect a grieving person to the energy of their loved one in the spirit world, a person's life can instantly change in a significantly positive way.

In the last twenty years or so, the world of mediumship has exploded. *Why?* I assume a very small portion of it is due to ego. It may also present an opportunity for so-called "mediums" to make money and commit evil. However, with the overwhelming amount of people who truly have spiritual gifts, who are using those God-given gifts to help others, this work is simply needed to make this world a better place. The need for mediumship work in this world is also increasing exponentially because many people fear "death," and many people fear the unknown. Besides the anecdotal information gathered from the tens of thousands of people who have reported having NDEs (convincing, nonetheless), we really can't truly know what happens to us until we leave our physical bodies ourselves for the final time.

The work of mediumship – two-way communication with spirit – can enlighten us as human beings. And it has done so for centuries, as evidenced in the Bible and in many other spiritual books. When someone truly believes in mediumship, and they believe that we truly don't die, faith increases. *Why?* Because once we acknowledge that we do not die, and we are part of something greater that lives forever, the fear of death subsides because there is no "end." You combine that with the overwhelming abundance of love that resonates from the spirit world, and you are "all good!" You can better accept God's plan as it unfolds, whether you like the plan or not.

I would like to sum up what I have learned from my experiences, research, and mediumship sessions, before you go on to read the five amazing, true, "goosebump raising" stories in the following chapters.

In my opinion, God is literally Love Itself. You are a spark of energy, or part of "God," that has chosen to experience "life" as a human being. You chose, as a soul, to experience every single thing that happens to you in this "reality." There is a blueprint and well-organized plan for each one of our lives. You have a destiny, but you also have free will, and they both work in conjunction to form your reality. (Please refer to chapter 9 in my first book). Each one of us has a very unique and special purpose in this world, but we have *all* come here to love unconditionally. We do not die. We just change form. You are energy and you cannot be created or destroyed. Your reality will simply change once your mission on Earth is complete. That consciousness – the true you, or your soul – will always experience some form of awareness, forever. In spirit, without your physical body, there is no fear, anger, jealousy, or any of the negative human emotions we create and experience here. You are love, you will always be love, and you can benefit by simply loving all things while you are here. Everything that shows up in your reality happens for a very specific reason that is often beyond our understanding. Embrace it, even when your life experience feels tragic or painful. Ask God for the opportunity to learn from your hardships and realize that when you transition to the next stage of your life, i.e., when you die and leave this physical body, it is simply another opportunity to love in the form that you are in, at that stage of your eternal existence.

CHAPTER 16

OH, BUDDY

Every so often, a mediumship session has a lasting effect on me that is beyond measure. It's not that any other session doesn't count or matter as much as any other. It's just that certain experiences hold a special place in my heart. It was one session with a woman named Jeni, whose nine-year-old son, "Buddy," transitioned Home, that I will cherish forever.

As I mentioned, on Monday nights, I often "go live" on Facebook to provide mediumship sessions and spiritual guidance to people who join the live online event. Over the last three years, this amazing, close-knit, spiritual community has grown to over 22,000 people. This community is full of beautiful and loving people, many who are grieving the loss of one or more loved ones. We go live for about two hours, and we don't just perform mediumship sessions. We pray, we share Scripture, and we discuss opportunities to spread more love in this world. On one particular Monday night in September 2020, we hosted a live event that would change hundreds, if not thousands, of lives forever.

Here is Jeni's story:

For Jeni, the birth of her first son was a long-awaited day. Jeni's first two children were girls, but her third child was going to be a boy! Jeni was looking forward to meeting her first son. On April 14, 2009, Jeni brought Braden, "Buddy," Patrick Miller into the world. The doctors and nurses quickly noted the incredible set of lungs Buddy possessed. He was a healthy, chubby, beautiful, eight-pound baby boy. "The sisters," as Buddy would eventually call them, were so excited to meet their new little brother.

For a moment in time, all the world was perfect for Jeni and their family. Then, an unexpected turn of events occurred as the doctors and nurses quickly became concerned with Buddy's breathing. As Jeni and her family started to grow concerned, Buddy was suddenly whisked away and taken to the Neonatal Intensive Care Unit (NICU). Buddy eventually recovered and grew to be a healthy boy with tons of energy.

As Buddy grew into a toddler, he continued to keep his family on their toes. A typical boy? Yes, and no. At a very young age, Buddy was attached to his mother, his dad, "the sisters," and extended family, more than a typical child. As Buddy grew older, the attachment increased. Buddy was constantly concerned and worried about everyone and he was never focused on himself. If Jeni had to choose one word to describe him, it would be "love." Anyone who looked into Buddy's bright blue eyes was captivated and they could also see his pure, innocent soul.

On January 11, 2017, the Miller's lives would change forever. While Jeni and her husband were at work, they both received a call from Buddy's school. The school said that Buddy had fallen, and the nurses stated that he was "off." The school requested that Buddy's parents were to pick him up immediately. When Jeni got to school to pick up Buddy, he looked and acted just fine. As the secretary and other staff shared the details about the fall and what had transpired that morning, Jeni began to grow extremely concerned, and fear started to set in for the entire Miller family. The school staff shared that Buddy had been playing basketball on the playground and suddenly he fell. He hit his head, was drooling, and his equilibrium was terribly off. The symptoms had subsided by the time Jeni and her husband sat with him in the nurse's office. Jeni and her husband took Buddy home as he continued to reassure them that he was okay.

For about two months prior to this event at school, Buddy's parents had been taking him to the doctors for stomach aches. The doctors were stumped as they ordered X-rays and ultrasounds that revealed no real answers. Buddy was also being treated for a lazy eye. Little did Jeni and her husband know that all these symptoms were leading them down a devastating road.

It wasn't until a subsequent emergency room visit that a diagnosis was revealed. That diagnosis ended up being the Miller's worst nightmare. As the doctors reviewed the MRI that was ordered, they requested an immediate transport for Buddy by ambulance to the children's hospital in Ann Arbor, Michigan. The Millers were then brought into a private room to receive the official diagnosis: Diffuse Intrinsic Pontine Glioma (DIPG). *The survival rate?* They were told it was less than 1%. The doctors instructed Jeni and her husband to "go home and make memories." They were informed that Buddy would pass before the end of the year. The doctors shared that there is no treatment for DIPG, outside of radiation, and that would only give them a "honeymoon" period.

To say that the Millers were devastated is a massive understatement. Here was this beautiful, loving, energetic boy who had his whole life in front of him, and at just seven years old he was given six to nine months to live.

Determined to prevent this diagnosis from becoming a reality, the Millers researched every resource they could to find an alternative solution to the one the doctors proposed. They did succeed in finding one such treatment option in Monterrey, Mexico. Friends, family, and the community, raised over $450,000 to make this experimental treatment a viable option. So, the Millers traveled to Mexico fifteen times in a twenty-one-month period to try to defy the odds. Jeni's slogan was, "Losing is not an option."

Unfortunately, on October 19, 2018, nine-year-old Braden "Buddy" Patrick Miller passed away. Buddy was able to spend the last year and a half of his short time on Earth, making magical memories with his entire family. The worst pain a parent can experience is having their child leave this world before they do. The Millers were now a family of four beautiful souls who had to navigate a road that no family ever wants to be on.

After the numbness wore off from the loss of Buddy, the "dark days" started to hit extremely hard for Jeni. She had convinced herself that through prayer, faith, and dedication to Buddy, he would be one of the 1% that would triumph from this devastating disease. To this very day, Jeni says that this reality is still hard for her to comprehend. Jeni says that every single day she feels like Buddy is just going to walk through the door. Not only was Buddy an amazing human being, he was, and is, an absolutely magical soul, not only to his family, but to the thousands of people who had the opportunity to get to know him while he was physically here with us. Life would never be the same for Jeni.

As a born-again Christian, Jeni always believed in God and had an interest in mediums and the afterlife. Jeni began following many Facebook pages for grieving mothers, listening to interviews with grieving parents, and she also started reading books about parents who have lost their own children. Jeni was grasping onto anything that would help ease her debilitating pain. Jeni desperately wanted to validate that Buddy was really in "Heaven," and that he was safe with God.

Jeni reached out to a local medium named Avianna, and although Avianna normally doesn't provide mediumship sessions prior to six months after someone passes, she agreed to do so, and she was able to connect with Buddy. Jeni was beyond grateful for this blessing.

Jeni's first session with Avianna was less than two months after Buddy's passing and it was beyond healing for her. "It was so comforting to receive these amazing messages," Jeni said later. Since Avianna offered meditation classes, Jeni felt it was a good idea to take them. As she started meditation, the pain from the loss was there, but she started to sense a feeling of peace that she could not explain. Unfortunately, bringing Buddy back was not an option, so she felt the next best thing would be to be able to connect to him herself through meditation and by raising her vibration.

One night while scrolling through Facebook, Jeni came across my Facebook page where I give free, live mediumship sessions. She felt an immediate connection and felt I was "a pure soul with positive intentions." A few minutes of experiencing the live event was all Jeni needed to confirm her thoughts. That evening I was speaking about faith, and I was focused on God's unconditional love for every single one of His children. "Love" is the very word Jeni uses to describe Buddy. She thought to herself, *A medium who believes in God, preaches love, and helps others?* Jeni was in, and she felt there was something very special here.

Jeni set an alarm on her phone to go off every Monday at 9:00 PM EST, so she could watch "Monday Night Live" faithfully week after week. Every Monday she hoped Buddy would come through, but as the weeks went on, Buddy was nowhere to be found. Jeni was so happy for the lucky viewers who were able to receive messages from their loved ones, but she often felt bummed. However, she believed that all things happen when they are supposed to, and she knew her time would come when God wanted it to.

As Jeni continued to watch on Monday nights, she found that watching others receive healing messages from their loved ones in spirit, allowed healing to transpire within herself. She was continuing her meditation practice and embracing every sign Buddy was able to send her from the "other side." It was one Monday evening in September 2020, that would forever change Jeni and her grief journey.

This particular evening, Jeni's heart started racing when I described the information I was obtaining from spirit. She understood all the details I was saying, but she was nervous, scared, and excited all at the same time. She knew, beyond a doubt, that it was Buddy coming through. Jeni typed the information she was validating in the chat box. She hesitated for a brief moment because of her nerves, but then she hit the send button in the chat. A few seconds after she sent in her comments, I asked her to send me her phone number. Jeni's heart dropped, she was shaking, and on the verge of panic, but in an excited way. She *knew* this was her son, and her excitement escalated along with her nerves.

I am going to let Jeni tell you the rest of the story in her own words.

From Jeni:

I hope you will take fifty minutes to listen and watch the incredible mediumship session I experienced that night with Daniel. It was so powerful, and I would be honored if you would watch the YouTube video of it here: https://youtu.be/alekNOmHTYw. Daniel was visibly affected by the intense connection he had with Buddy.

The validations were absolutely mind-blowing and completely undeniable. From Buddy's Snoopy doll, to his eyes, to the song, 'Livin' On A Prayer,' by Bon Jovi, no reasonable person could deny that Buddy was with Daniel during that session. I knew for a fact it was Buddy sending messages to me through Daniel!

Even though most things Daniel said were immediately validated, there were a few things during the session that I could not understand. However, each one of those things was validated quickly after the session when I wasn't so nervous. It is difficult to fully grasp all the details when you are in a mediumship session. For this reason, I was so grateful the session was recorded. I can't even count how many times I have listened to it. The connection Daniel and Buddy had during this time was overwhelming and was felt by the nearly four-hundred people watching their powerful connection.

The following day I received an inbox message from Daniel asking if he could call me. My heart sank as I wondered if Daniel had additional messages for me. Did Buddy share something with him that he was uncomfortable speaking about in front of the group online? I quickly responded, but I was a little anxious. My phone rang, I answered, and Daniel was on the other end.

'I don't know why I am calling you, but I just felt I needed to,' Daniel said. He stated that he simply wanted to speak with me because Buddy was so powerful. Daniel stated that Buddy was so strong, and his soul was still with him energetically.

Buddy is such a special soul that I have had multiple people tell me how he positively influenced their lives, even when many of those people never physically met Buddy. Daniel is one of them. Even as I write this, over one year later, guess who is still with Daniel all the time? Yup. . .Buddy!

After that phone call, over the next year, Daniel and I stayed in touch, and a friendship was formed. We became Facebook friends, and I began to follow him and his beautiful family on social media. At this point I feel as though I have known him and his family for my whole life.

Daniel and I kept in touch. He would randomly send me messages when Buddy was communicating with him. My heart melted each time I read those messages from Daniel. I have received so many signs, symbols, and messages from Buddy, so I am not surprised anymore, but these communications just further confirm what I already know.

I'm like most other people in that I am a "believer," but I still have a little skepticism about the afterlife. I am often asked about the experience with Daniel and all the other experiences I have had with Buddy since he has passed, because there are so many of them to share. To this day I love sharing the session I had with Daniel and all the other moments I have had with Buddy even without a 'medium.'

Thank you, Daniel, for increasing my faith in God, helping me better understand Buddy's purpose, and thank you for being true to the gifts that God is asking you to use to help others like me.

—Jeni

CHAPTER 17

NOT JUST A KAREN

Since I have been conducting the work of mediumship for many years, I've had the honor of meeting some pretty amazing people. I have built several long-lasting relationships with people I would not have had the opportunity and pleasure of meeting if it were not for this amazing gift. It was a woman named Karen who would change my perspective on this whole mediumship thing. I sometimes forget the power of spirit, and I laugh when we, as humans, think we can even begin to understand what the Universe has planned for our lives here on Earth. Karen and her family will always hold a special place in my heart. Here is their story:

In early January of 2020, the Pierson family reached out to me because they were severely grieving the sudden loss of David, their fifty-nine-year-old husband and father. The family was getting together a week or so after I received the e-mail, and even though I was booked out for months, I was inspired to offer their family a mediumship session sooner than my calendar offered. I opened an appointment for them, and they immediately booked a phone session for their entire family.

It turns out that Karen (the mother and wife), and her daughter, April, had watched our show "Monday Night Live" together on Facebook for well over a year prior to booking the appointment. They really liked the live mediumship sessions, and they loved the healing that Monday Night Live (MNL) provided for so many. Karen was a "top fan," and a big supporter of me and my mission.

On January 10, 2020, during a mediumship session with me, the Piersons were able to connect to their father, David, in spirit. He had many validating, powerful messages for his entire family. The messages were specific, accurate, and so full of love! Even though they would rather have had David physically there with them, they settled for an abundance of healing messages from him via connecting through a medium. The session provided so much healing, comfort, and faith for their entire family.

Over the next weeks and months following the session, Karen would e-mail or message me with more validations from our meeting. She continued to show an abundance of love and support for me and for this work. In the Fall of 2020, Karen and her family wanted to schedule another session with me for David's birthday, which was on May 24, 2021. Since I do not offer private sessions on Mondays, they booked the next day, Tuesday, May 25, 2021. They booked the session eight months in advance because it was a special day for them. I offered Karen the opportunity to move up her appointment several times, but she insisted on keeping it for that day.

On May 24, 2021, the day before their long-awaited session, Karen made her way to each of her children to celebrate their dad's birthday. Even though Karen was grieving the loss of her husband, she took the time to bring flowers and a balloon to every single one of her children. Then, Karen and her daughter, April, visited David's grave and enjoyed dinner together that evening. At dinner, they had the opportunity to share memories of Karen's late husband, and the children's father, David, on his birthday, even though he was not physically there to celebrate with them. With many hugs and kisses, April dropped her mom off at home.

Less than an hour later, April received a phone call that would change her life forever. Karen was having a heart attack and she needed to be rushed to the hospital immediately. Just one hour earlier, April and her mother were enjoying dinner together on David's birthday, and now suddenly, Karen was being mercy-flighted to the hospital. As she was being loaded into the helicopter, Karen adamantly reminded the entire family about her session with me the next night. Her daughter, Tiffany, said her mom was insistent upon her family keeping the appointment that Karen booked for the day after David's birthday. David Jr., Krystal, and the rest of the family assured their mother that one way or another, they would not miss the appointment.

I received a Facebook message from Karen's daughter, Tiffany, on May 25th. The message read: "Daniel, this is Tiffany, Karen's daughter. We had an emergency last night with mom. Can I contact you later today? She had a session set up with you for this evening."

I reached out to Tiffany and discovered that the news was not good. In the early hours of May 25, 2021, Karen Pierson took her last breath. Karen passed away the day after her husband's birthday. She passed away on the same day she was to have a mediumship session (with many other earlier appointments available to her), to experience a connection with her late husband in spirit. Little did Karen, or anyone else, know that she would pass away the same day as her mediumship appointment which she had made more than eight months prior.

I remember asking Tiffany if she still wanted to keep the appointment, and with severe shock and grief, she said, "Daniel, who gets to have an appointment with a medium the same day their mom passes away?" I couldn't agree more, especially because her mom was the one who booked the appointment so long ago.

With about fifteen people on a video conference call, we conducted a ninety-minute mediumship session for many members of the Pierson family. *And guess who came through strongly and accurately? You guessed it. Karen!* The session was so full of love, and it provided the family so much peace and understanding.

Through me, Karen "went around the room" with messages for almost everyone attending. To this day, the family expresses their gratitude for such an amazing experience that Karen was able to provide to her family. I feel that somehow, some way, Karen's soul knew she would pass away that day, and this was her way to immediately connect with her family.

Who books a session with a medium eight months in advance, passes away the same day as the scheduled session, and then powerfully connects with her entire family from the spirit world through the medium? *Karen Pierson does!*

Here are a few thoughts from Karen's daughter, Tiffany:

Daniel John has truly changed my life. When my dad passed away, my sister mentioned that she followed a medium named Daniel, and that we should reach out to him. Daniel had a long waiting list and a full schedule, but he felt compelled to have a phone session with my family (Mom, me, and my three siblings).

That session, with my dad in spirit, was well over an hour long and it truly felt like we were having a clear conversation with my father. From mentioning my parents' wedding anniversary, to speaking about playing Tic Tac Toe with my brother when he was younger, to talking in detail about a toy train I had just purchased for my daughter, my father was strong in his communication with us through Daniel. Every validation proved to us that my dad was still with us. I truly felt like a different person after that night. I felt better equipped to move forward in life knowing my dad was right by my side. After that amazing reading, my mom scheduled another session with Daniel.

This next session was to be the day after my dad's birthday. Mom wanted to celebrate Dad's special day together as a family. Daniel attempted to reschedule that session a few times, but Mom insisted on keeping the day. Tragically, my mom passed away in the early morning hours of that very day (the day after my dad's birthday, which is the day she scheduled the session for).

I contacted Daniel to let him know the situation. While Mom was in the hospital the evening before she passed, she specifically told us not to forget the reading with Daniel. I contacted Daniel, informed him of my mom's passing, and explained that we still wanted to have the session with him.

I think Daniel was a bit hesitant on hosting another session with our family because he could not guarantee Mom would come through so soon after passing. However, Daniel immediately started receiving messages from my mom. After over an hour and a half of consistent validation from our mother in spirit, on a day in which she insisted on having a mediumship session, we experienced an abundance of peace knowing she was still able to give us every blessing she possibly could, even from the 'other side.'

During that session with Daniel, my mom seemed to give each one of my family members exactly the love they needed. These messages ranged from reminding my niece how amazing she is and how she should keep her head up, to exclaiming how my nephew is going to be a special type of leader, to telling me that I would now be the rock for everyone throughout the difficult processes ahead, to reciting an actual conversation my sister and I had privately in the hospital the night my mom passed away.

My mother was such a faith-filled woman, and she had such a strong belief and passion for what Daniel does. In the session with my mom, she reminded us how happy she is and how she will show us she is still here with us. In the hospital the evening before she passed away, she told us to look for the signs, and I must say, the consistent signs she sends remind me that our souls are so deeply connected, and that love will always keep us bonded in this life and in the next.

Since the sessions with Daniel, I have been asking Mom for specific signs, and at the same time, keeping my mind open to receiving those signs. I truly feel as though Daniel opened a doorway in order to allow me to connect daily with my mom – my very best friend – on a soul level. And for that I could not be more grateful. Without that connection and reassurance, I honestly don't know how deeply I would be consumed in my grief. Thank you, Daniel, Mom, Dad, and God, for allowing and facilitating the beautiful connection of our souls so we may be better able to continue to grow here on Earth and expand beyond the physical world.

–Tiffany

CHAPTER 18

QUITE A HOME RUN

Ever since my son, Sammy, was one year old, he has absolutely loved baseball. In June 2021, I was at the little league fields watching Sammy's baseball game. Even though he was only eight years old at the time, Sam had quite the skills and a natural ability to play ball. At a game against the rival team from Waterloo, New York, Sammy was up to bat. I always capture Sammy's "at bats" on video so we can work on his swing, but also so we always have the memories. As I hit the record button on the camera, the pitch was delivered. Sammy hit the hardest ball he had ever hit up to that point in his young career. Needless to say, my reaction was one for the record books. He hit that ball so hard that the fielder didn't get to it until Sam was on second base. It was a home run! At that moment, I could not have been prouder of that kid! All the backyard baseball practice paid off. As he rounded the bases the smile on my face continued to grow.

Because I was so proud of him, and because it was such a monster hit, of course I had to make a TikTok video of it. I posted the video and didn't think much of it. A few hours later, I checked my phone and saw an abundance of notifications from TikTok. Apparently, Sammy's hit was absolutely amazing, but also, many people were quite amused by my rather obnoxious reaction to his home run. The video went viral! It had over 250,000 views in the first 24 hours. People were commenting on so many things. It was fun, and we all enjoyed reading the comments.

A few days later, with the video at well over 500,000 views, ESPN SportsCenter sent me a private message asking my permission to post the video on their Instagram page. We obliged and over a seven-day period, that video had over four million views on many different platforms. It was **quite an amazing experience!**

A day after we posted the video, I received a message on TikTok from a woman who was immersed in severe grief. I typically receive anywhere from two to five messages or e-mails a day from people who simply need help because of their severe grief. This woman was no different. Sarah had lost her son, Mason, just two months earlier and she was struggling to survive. The pain of losing Mason obviously devastated her, and she was desperate to connect with her son.

She started off by asking if I had any appointments available, to which I responded that my calendar was full and that I would gladly recommend a few other mediums. However, as I recommended some other mediums to her, I started to receive messages from the spirit world. I often don't know who the spirit is, or what they want to "talk" about, but we quickly discovered that Sarah's son, Mason, wasn't waiting for a preset appointment with a medium to communicate with his mother.

The messages started with a Sesame Street® symbol, to which she quickly answered that she recently gave Mason's Elmo towel as a baby shower gift to his son. As we both started to get goosebumps, I could not hold back what I believed to be Mason's spirit was sharing with me. Mason then confirmed that his "accident" was no accident, and that his passing was the way it was "supposed to be." He continued by showing me "GI Joe®," which usually is my symbol for "military."

When Sarah couldn't validate the military man, or the "J" name like "Joe," I asked if it could simply be a reference to camouflage. She stated that Mason wore "camo" all the time and that his "camo" shorts were still sitting in a pile of clothes on the front steps of his house at the time. "Camouflage" was also confirmed three months later when Mason's cousin, Julian (a "J" name like "Joe"), successfully completed boot camp. It was Mason's way to let his close friend and cousin know he was proud of him.

I then asked Sarah, "Who is the little girl who is under/around five years old?" She replied that Mason had been very close to his stepdaughter, Elainah, who was five years old at the time of his passing. Sarah also expressed that Elainah really missed Mason. Sarah later confirmed that Elainah actually sees Mason's spirit, so this was his way to confirm that she really does see his energy.

At this point, I started to believe it truly was Mason trying to communicate with his mother through me. He wanted to tell his mom that "she didn't mess anything up." He wanted to tell her that "nothing could change the plan." He shared that it is "awesome" where he is, and that it "sucks for you to be there on Earth." "That was his personality," Sarah said. Mason told me to tell her that he is "A-okay." I don't usually hear that, so I told her that an "A" name must be significant. It turns out Mason's son's name is Aiden, and Mason also has a brother named Antonio.

Mason told me to tell his mom to smile because he is smiling. Mason shared with her that all will work out and he told his mother not to overthink things. He kept making me feel like I wanted to talk about his smile and Sarah confirmed that he had "the greatest smile." In fact, Mason's father always said that Mason had a "1,000-watt smile."

Mason then mentioned something that would later almost prove that it was him. "Toothpicks," I wrote to Sarah on TikTok chat. Sarah said she could not understand that reference. Throughout a typical mediumship session, there are many things that don't make sense right away. I never question spirit, and I always honor the energy and the message. I continued by letting her know that Mason was telling her to smile and to not lose her faith.

Sarah stated that she was angry at God, and she felt like Mason's passing was a huge slap in the face. I was inspired to suggest a book for Sarah to read which was, "Good Grief," by Theresa Caputo. She said she would read it as she thanked me for my time. I told her that I hoped the messages helped her and she responded with, "More than you know."

If you are wondering what Sammy's TikTok video has to do with Sarah and her son, Mason, I will tell you now.

After the completion of Sarah's impromptu session, she felt compelled to let me know how she "found" me. She told me that Sammy's home run video popped up on her TikTok "for you" page. The "for you" page is the feed where TikTok "randomly" shows you videos that the algorithm thinks you may enjoy based on many criteria. Out of the hundreds of millions of videos that TikTok could "randomly" show her, it was Sammy's home run video that stopped Sarah in her tracks.

As she watched the video, she noticed something very interesting. Mason played baseball too, and not only was Mason talented as well, Sammy and Mason had another thing in common. Sammy wore number "6" on his team jersey that year and their uniforms were blue with yellow lettering. One of Sarah's favorite pictures of Mason is from when he was playing baseball. *What colors were Mason's uniform and what number did he wear in the photo?* You guessed it. It was a blue jersey with yellow lettering, and, of course, Mason wore "#6!" I could not believe it! Sarah felt compelled to tell me how she found me, and that Mason was responsible for this "coincidence" from the "other side." *How amazing is that?*

What about the toothpicks? Two days later, Sarah messaged me with the validation. It turns out that Mason's girlfriend had a conversation with Mason (in spirit), about leaving the toothpicks out on the counter. When Sarah told Mason's girlfriend that a medium told her something about the toothpicks, she turned white. They were both absolutely amazed!

That wasn't the end of Mason's ability to communicate with his mother through a medium. About two months after our first impromptu mediumship session, **one of Sarah's videos popped up on *my* TikTok page.** I messaged her on TikTok chat to tell her that I was sorry for her loss. I didn't even know it was her until our previous messages came up in the chat. After I recognized that she was the one I gave the random mediumship session to a few months prior, I felt Mason starting to come through for his mother again. After asking, and receiving permission from her to pass on messages, Mason again came through strongly and deliberately.

Mason started off by telling Sarah that he messes with her electronics. He then shared with her that although he can feel her pain, he can also feel the abundance of love she constantly sends him. Mason was relaying so much information that I had to call her on the phone so I could share it with her with more detail and accuracy that I could over Internet chat. I called Sarah, and Mason came through even more loudly and clearly.

During the impromptu phone session, Mason provided about twenty validations for his mom. From specific names of friends/family that Mason was concerned with here in the physical world, to the details about the eternal connection that Mason and his mother have had over many lifetimes, Mason's communication came through so beautifully.

Throughout an approximate one-hour phone call with Sarah, Mason was able to pass on many powerful messages to his mother through me. After the session, Sarah could breathe more easily, and she was beyond grateful for the blessing of being able to reconnect with her son. Mason even came through again via TikTok messenger when I reached back out to Sarah to ask what her feelings were about putting her and Mason's story in this book. **This young man is so amazing!**

Here is a message from Sarah:

My name is Sarah Suschank and Mason Christopher Lilledahl is my first-born son. I lost him in a car accident on April 10, 2021. I can tell you there is no pain that compares to this. Mason is the most beautiful soul you can imagine, and everyone loves his energy. Since his passing, I had been dissociating for a few months by endlessly watching social media from my bed. In June, I was stopped in my tracks by a video that I could have sworn was my son playing baseball. Same exact number '6,' same team colors, blue and yellow, only the kid was much younger, but it was obviously enough to catch my attention and click on the creator's page. To my surprise, this man was a medium.

I had been searching for a medium to connect me with my son. I felt as though Mason was telling me to reach out to Daniel, so I did. Unfortunately, Daniel was booked for the rest of the year, but he was kind enough to give me several messages over the next six months on a few different occasions. Daniel's gift is what has saved me from the pit I was drowning in.

Almost all Daniel's messages 'hit home' for Mason and me. Daniel talked about Mason's son, and he told me things only Mason would know. I have pages of notes from sessions with Daniel of what Mason was telling me. Anytime I really needed to hear from Mason, I would somehow reconnect with Daniel. It was almost as if Mason knew I needed him, and he was able to count on Daniel to find me.

There is absolutely nothing that can make losing a child easier, but Daniel has made it much more bearable. My son and I have such a strong soul connection that losing him was like losing myself. When I can communicate with Mason through Daniel, I can breathe just a little easier.

—Sarah

CHAPTER 19

A PRETTY "SWEET" EXPERIENCE

There is a Divine plan for every single thing we experience here on Earth, and that plan is often beyond our comprehension. Since practicing the work of mediumship, I have had experiences that simply don't make sense logically. I have had encounters with people and experienced situations that are nothing short of miracles. These divinely guided circumstances have led me to an understanding that we simply can't fully grasp the power of the Holy Spirit, and we can't fully grasp what God's plan is for our lives. It was one night in Sacramento in January 2022, that would prove to be one of those examples of something you just can't make up.

While in California, as we were filming for a media project, two of my best friends and I had a day off to enjoy the city of Sacramento. While looking online for events to attend in the city, I saw that John Edward – one of the most well-known mediums in the world – was having an event that evening. *What are the chances that another medium from New York would be in Sacramento the same night we had a free evening during our filming?*

As I visited John's website, I was disappointed to find out that the event was sold out. I knew it was a long shot, but I sent John an Instagram message asking him if we could purchase three tickets for the event even though it was completely sold out. I sent the message and figured we would just find something else to do.

As we continued our morning activities, enjoying our free time, I received a message on Instagram. It was John Edward, or one of his staff. The message stated that we were welcome to come to the event and that we would be John's special guests! *What are the chances of that?* Needless to say, even though my friends were a little tired of all the "medium stuff" that occurred while we were in Sacramento, we all decided to attend the event because it was an opportunity we couldn't pass up.

When we arrived at the hotel where the event was taking place, we decided to grab a quick drink. As we approached the bar, a woman noticed and then commented about Buddy's DIPG bracelet that I was wearing on my wrist. (Buddy from Chapter 16 in this book). Because I didn't want to make it awkward as a medium attending another medium's event, I simply stated that the bracelet was in memory of a young boy named Buddy who had passed away. This woman quickly volunteered the information that her son had also passed away. As I told her I was sorry for her loss, I started to get that familiar feeling on/in my body when spirit is starting to come through.

Because I was at another medium's event, I did not want to advertise that I am a medium as well, but I could not hold back the impressions I was receiving. I quietly shared with the woman, Debbie, that I am a medium and I asked her permission to share with her what I was receiving.

After about twenty minutes of many tears and even some laughter, Debbie was able to feel and validate the energy of her son, Austin. Austin was able to provide me with names, numbers, and specific details about his passing. There is no way I could have known these details by any ordinary means. Even as a self-admitted skeptic, Debbie said she felt lighter after our meeting. We exchanged phone numbers and kept in touch.

Debbie texted me later that evening. She told me that she and her daughter validated the few things they could not initially understand during the impromptu session we had earlier that night. Even though it was a little uncomfortable giving a mediumship session at another medium's event, I knew it was meant to be because of all the circumstances that led up to that moment.

Over the next few weeks Debbie would randomly text me with more validations from our meeting. She found me on Facebook and started to follow my page. On January 31, 2022, Debbie texted me to ask me what "Monday Night Live" was. I explained to her what we do on Monday nights on Facebook, and I didn't think any more about it. As we were live on Facebook that night, the first mediumship session was for a woman who had lost her three-year-old son. It was a very heavy session, but it seemed to provide her some relief and hope, even though she had experienced such a tragic physical loss. As I started to get the "clues" for the next energy that wanted to connect with their loved one, I noticed that a woman named Debbie was connecting with everything I was saying. As I looked at her name, I realized it was that same woman whom I had met in Sacramento. *No way!*

I called Debbie on the phone while live on Facebook and her deceased son, Austin, immediately made his presence known. Validation after validation, it was clear that Austin was coming through strongly for his mother. Debbie said that it was something she really needed at that point in her life. Between the session in

Sacramento and the session on Facebook, Debbie was better able to start and then continue her healing process.

What if John Edward never wrote me back and invited us to be his guests? What if we didn't grab a drink before the event? There are so many "what ifs." This is exactly how the Universe works, and "It" is always perfect. The less you question what happens in your life, and the more you trust what shows up in your reality, the more enjoyable life can be. The more you understand that life happens for *you, not* to *you, opportunities to experience unconditional love will find their way into your reality.*

Here is a message from Debbie:

Austin was my only son, and he is the first male grandson of the Sweet family. He was born in 1997, and grew up in Roseville, California. He was one of the most adored friends to many people in our town. I proudly raised Austin and my daughter, Ashley, as a single mom. I worked hard to give them a quality life while putting myself through nursing school with the goal of becoming an emergency and critical care nurse.

Austin grew up with a natural gift to make friends easily. He had a compassion for animals and cared for all creatures. Austin was a selfless young man with an infectious sense of humor. In 2019, Austin moved into his first apartment with his girlfriend and one of his childhood friends. Unfortunately, that move would lead to an outcome no one ever expected.

On July 13, 2019, my son Austin Sweet was murdered by a man who was supposed to be his friend and roommate. It was an experience that I would not wish on my worst enemy. I could not understand why this had to happen.

At his funeral service Austin was remembered as a kind and giving friend with an amazing sense of humor. To Austin's friends his name was, 'Sweet,' rereferring not only to his last name but to his personality as well.

After Austin's death, I often found myself struggling with finding some sort of peace and understanding about this whole situation. I questioned if Austin was really 'alive in a spirit world.' I was searching for a connection, and I was hungry for signs that my baby was still with me. It was a struggle to live without him and every day was a constant battle to be able to comprehend the fact that I had to live my life without my only son. Over the next year and a half, I would struggle to make sense of it all. The pain was absolutely unbearable.

In January 2022, approximately two years after Austin's passing, my daughter, Ashley, and I attended an event hosted by psychic medium John Edward. Of course, I wanted to connect with Austin, but there was a significant amount of skepticism in me about this whole 'mediumship' thing. This was the second time I had ever been to an event like this, but this one felt different. After finding our seats, we felt compelled to go sit at the bar for a drink, even though we agreed earlier that this night would not be a 'drinking kind of night.'

While having our drink, three men approached the bar next to us. The two men were making fun of the other one for ordering a soda water and we thought that was funny. I would never have expected that my view of the afterlife would significantly start to change at that very moment.

The man next to me apologized for 'being in my bubble,' as I laughed and welcomed him in. I noticed he was wearing a neon green wristband. I asked him what that wristband represented, and he responded that it was in memory of a child who had passed away. I immediately felt the need to tell him that I also lost my child. At that exact moment, I felt a flood of energy run through me and I experienced extreme emotions as the man started to talk.

This man told me his name was Daniel and he explained that he was a medium. He explained that even though he didn't want to step on the toes of the medium we were visiting, he felt overwhelmed to pass on a message from my son. He asked my permission, and I agreed to hear what Daniel had to say, even though I was still a skeptic about mediums at that point. Although I had a difficult time understanding what Daniel was saying because of my skepticism, my daughter was overwhelmed with emotion from my son's presence.

The very first thing Daniel said was that he was getting the impression to mention an 'artichoke' of all things. I was shocked, because our family absolutely loves artichokes and we used to fight over the hearts at the dinner table. Daniel then brought up the name, 'Robert.' We recently had dinner with my brother-in-law, Rob, and he actually gave me his artichoke heart. We figured out that Austin was validating that he truly was communicating with Daniel because, unfortunately, Austin was stabbed in the heart, which is what led to his passing. There is no way Daniel would have known that. This was Austin's way to make sure we knew it was him, and that he was with us at dinner that evening when Rob gave me his artichoke heart!

Then, Daniel brought up the name, 'Will.' Will was Austin's very first friend when we moved to Roseville. Austin called Will his little brother and was very protective of him. Then Daniel kept bringing up the number '23,' and I insisted that I knew nothing about a 23. On our way home, we realized that Will just celebrated his 23rd birthday. Daniel said that Austin wanted us to reach out to Will, so after we validated Will's actual age, it was double validation for us to connect with Will.

Daniel asked my daughter, Ashley, if at one time she and Austin had a distant relationship but then became very close again. Without knowing who the woman next to me was, he asked if she was related to my son. Ashley told Daniel that she was Austin's sister, and said, yes, they had a time where they were distant, but then were very close.

Daniel described Austin as funny, and at times even 'inappropriately funny.' I couldn't agree more and that made me smile. Daniel brought up a 'dog' and then something about the 'chocolate.' This made a lot of sense because Austin had a dog named Roxy who was his pride and joy. Austin was killed on Roxy's birthday, and unfortunately just eight months later, Roxy passed away one week after Austin's birthday on the 23rd. (There is the '23' again). When Roxy was a puppy, she ate all of Austin's Halloween chocolates which put her in the doggie ICU for two days. Austin was devastated because he thought he killed his dog. We realized this was Austin's way to let us know he was with Roxy in Heaven.

After receiving more validations and messages from Austin, I was in awe. It took weeks to process it all, but to say I was a little less of a skeptic after my impromptu session with Daniel would be an understatement.

Daniel and I exchanged numbers as I thanked him for connecting me with my son, Austin, in the spirit world, even though I didn't understand how it all worked. After that night, I searched for Daniel on Facebook and found that he has a page where he 'goes live' on Monday nights and provides free mediumship sessions for people.

While watching Daniel one night on Facebook, I was again blessed with a very unexpected mediumship session from Daniel. Daniel gave the clues, 'Deb,' '13,' and the name 'Tyler.' With over three-hundred people on the live feed, my heart raced when I realized this could be for me. My name is Debbie, but my friends call me 'Deb,' Austin was killed on the 13th, and my daughter's fiancée's name is Tyler. I literally thought my heart was going to explode. The pounding in my chest was something I can't even come close to describing. At that point, I had no doubt that this information was for me. I wrote in the chat how I resonated with the information, and Daniel asked for my phone number and for my permission to share with me what he was receiving.

Here we go again! Daniel asked about either the name, 'Chip,' or if I recently ate chocolate chips. I was flabbergasted. As I sat on my couch listening to the previous person receiving a message from their loved one, I was eating homemade ice cream with chocolate chips. I couldn't even remember the last time I had chocolate chips.

He also asked about sliced turkey and if I ate a sub recently. There is absolutely no way he could have known that I just finished eating sliced turkey and cheese. This was Austin's way of letting me know he was with me. At that moment, my heart was so full of love, and I experienced an abundance of emotion.

Daniel brought up that Austin was aware of something being planned for him at my daughter's wedding. He said that multiple people were going back and forth on what should be done, and that they would 'all win.' Daniel also mentioned a heart and key piece of jewelry, like a locket. At the time, I wasn't aware of anything being planned, but after my session with Daniel, I called my daughter, Ashley. When I told her what Austin said through Daniel, she immediately broke into tears. Ashley told me they were planning a couple of things to do in memory of Austin, but they hadn't concluded what they would do yet. She said she hadn't told me because she didn't want to make me cry. My daughter's friend had planned on giving Ashley a heart-shaped locket with a key attached to a safety pin to attach to her bridal bouquet. I had no knowledge of these things, but Austin was able to share that information with Daniel.

After the session with Daniel, I shared my experience with my mother who enlightened me with an important piece of information that I was unable to connect with at the time of the session. Daniel had mentioned the name 'Roy,' 'Pepsi®', and a 'piano.' I was so overwhelmed with emotion while thinking of my son, that I completely blocked out the fact that my maternal grandfather is named Roy! Grandpa Roy gave me piano lessons as a child, and he even bought a piano for my sister and me. And by the way, my mother was a 'Pepsiholic.' I have no memories of my mom from my childhood without a Pepsi® in her hand. This was my grandfather's way of saying, 'Hi,' to me and to my mom, while also letting us know that Grandpa Roy was there for Austin when he passed.

I often struggle with faith, but my experiences with Daniel helped open a door that has been tightly locked since the murder of my son. After the sessions with Daniel, I feel like my healing process has started. Although I would rather have Austin here with me physically, I am starting to understand that there is a bigger picture that I am not aware of. My heart has been opened to so many things and now I'm not afraid to acknowledge what the Universe has to offer me and my family.

I am often very selective as to with whom I share my story, but I was compelled to share it with a grieving coworker who recently lost her mother and brother. Like I was, she had been struggling, but only days after my experience, she 'randomly' shared with me that she felt like she may want to contact a medium. When I told her my story she broke down into tears and felt 'this was her answer' to move forward with her search for the right medium. Now she will hopefully be able to feel the absolute love, healing, and increased faith in something greater, like I was able to experience by opening my heart and mind to something I didn't understand.

–Debbie

CHAPTER 20

JUST IN THE "NICK" OF TIME

There are times in our lives when we experience significantly defining moments. Sometimes it's a graduation or a wedding, and sometimes it is realizing you are a medium who has a gift you can use to help others heal by connecting them with their loved ones who have passed away. When I first discovered this gift, I would never have imagined that mediumship would lead me to some of the most amazing experiences I have ever had. On April 2, 2022, I experienced yet another one of those defining moments that left me and many others in awe.

As I went for a walk on April 1, 2022, I was randomly thinking about my editor for this book, Dyan. I realized she sent me her edit a few weeks prior and I had not sent her anything back. About thirty seconds after I had that thought, she texted me, requesting an update. I told her I had been busy with the kids and would get her some of my edits very soon. I then texted her and told her that I felt like I wanted to add more content to the book, but I felt like it may be content about things that had not yet happened. She agreed, and we left it at that. As I returned home after my walk, my wife and I did our nightly routine with the kids, then we spent some quality time together and went to sleep. What happened next, still blows my mind to this very day.

That night, I had an extremely vivid dream that I was delivering a mediumship session to a family who was grieving the loss of their son. He was impressing thoughts in my mind just like a mediumship session in "real life." The dream was extremely vivid, and I was truly feeling the emotions of the family and the energy of the young man in spirit. As I awoke, I quickly realized I was dreaming, but still felt that I obtained a large amount of information from this young man in spirit. As I tried to go back to sleep, I felt a nudge from this young man to get up and go write down what I remembered from the dream. I remember joking with him saying, *Dude, I'll remember. Just let me go back to sleep.* He insisted I get up and write down what I remembered, so after I felt a jolt, I did just that. After writing down all the details I could recall, I went back to sleep.

As I woke up later that morning, I quickly remembered what had transpired just a few hours prior. As quickly as I could think, *What am I going to do with this information?* A follow-up thought of, *Put it on Facebook so you can find the family,* instantly followed. After questioning the entire thing, I realized how strong and powerful the experience was. I had goosebumps the entire time I was writing the information down and I was also getting extremely emotional. I put all doubt aside, listened to my intuition, and at 8:26 AM on April 2, 2022, I posted the following information (this is the original post):

"A young man in spirit needs your help!!
Last night, I had an extremely vivid dream that inspired me to post this.
I was awakened VERY early this morning by a young man in spirit who needs our help contacting his family!
Why he can't reach out to them directly is part of the mystery of this whole mediumship thing I may never understand.
Either way. . . he needs our help.
Would you help us?
Here are the details he shared with me.

I am hoping we can find this grieving family!

Details:
—A young male 18-22 (approximately)
—He and his (most likely) girlfriend, passed very quickly, and most likely in a tragedy.
—He has a big loving family (4-5 siblings) (mostly girls).
—I get the name, "David" (2 generations), an E name like "Ed," or "Ethan," and an A name like "Anna" (this is a younger sister of his). Also, H name (like "Howard"), M (like "Maddie").
—He tells me there is a boat involved but didn't necessarily attribute to his passing.
—The family feels very Christian, and he makes me feel like they have mixed feelings about mediums.
—Oprah Winfrey has something to do with their family.
—He must have been tall.
—Pig reference (Porky or Peppa), or police officer (Sorry). Both may mean something significant!

Here are private details that you may or may not know about the family/situation:
—Frankenstein/ Franken Berry® cereal
—Gumballs are a big deal
—One of the young daughters recently tried wine
—His teeth are okay, and his smile is gleaming
—HE IS "A-OK," and in "Heaven""

When I tell you that within two hours, we found this young man's family through social media, I am not kidding you. It turns out that another medium in California had been working with a family who seemed to fit many of the details listed above. The medium, whose name is Ellie, put a group chat together with me, her, and the mother and sister of who she thought this young man in spirit was. As we started to chat, it seemed pretty evident that it surely was the son and brother of these two women. I agreed to call them as soon as I could. An hour later I picked up the phone to make that call.

To be clear, this type of situation does not happen very often. This dream experience was brand new territory for me. I had never been awakened from a dream, pushed to write down what I experienced, post it on Facebook when I got up, and then proceed to call a grieving family who may or may not be connected to this young man who visited me in my dream. One would think it would be an awkward phone call, but it was quite the opposite.

I started off the call stating to the family, on speaker phone, that although much of the information that was posted on Facebook seemed to fit with their family and with their son in spirit, we had to do our due diligence to make sure it was truly him. I told them about who I am and expressed my sympathy to their family. I also shared that I like to pray and protect all parties before we engage in spirit communication, and they obliged. I explained the process of how mediumship works for me, and I asked them to validate the information from the Facebook post. As soon as Amy, the mother of the young man in spirit, started talking, I immediately began to receive strong impressions. She validated about 90% of the information from the Facebook post and the rest is history.

As it turned out, after approximately one hour on the phone, a young man named, "Nick," got his wish from the "other side." Nick was able to use me as a medium to communicate with his family on an extremely high level.

Nick helped me describe his personality to his family for validation, and he was crystal clear with his communication. Nick communicated about oranges and his love for fruit, and he was able to validate the name of the young man who passed away in the accident with him. Nick was able to pass on messages to many people in the family, and he validated many current events and names of close friends and family. Nick is a force to be reckoned with and the love he has for his family overwhelmed me. I am usually pretty controlled emotionally during mediumship sessions, even though I am an emotional guy, but this experience was different.

As we progressed through the session, Nick shifted the focus to his father. Through me, Nick shared in detail how his dad was grieving in a very specific way. Nick mentioned the beers he'd had with his dad, acknowledged he was "okay," and relayed the fact that he understood how his dad was struggling with his faith. I could feel the emotion through the phone, and I had trouble holding it together.

At the completion of the call, Gabby (Nick's sister), David (Nick's father), and Amy (Nick's mother), validated much of what Nick had communicated to them through me. The amount of love and uplifting energy that transpired in that call is beyond explanation. To say that the family felt a significant wave of peace and love from connecting with their son in spirit, is a gigantic understatement. I was emotional and felt Nick thanking me and encouraging me to continue doing this work, regardless of what anyone else thinks. His energy is so full of love, and he left an impression on me that will last forever.

As I went through the rest of the day with my kids, I could not stop thinking about this grieving family and what had transpired earlier that day. Since that was the first experience I had when spirit came to me in a dream like that, it was hard to comprehend. Just like all the other stages of this journey, I don't question God's plan anymore. I just trust it. I don't try to understand the Universe's plan, because I feel we can't completely understand God's likeness while in this human body due to our limited minds and restricted understanding. The more you trust in something greater, the more you can live a life filled with love! I will let Amy and her family tell you a little more about Nick from the time he was born, up to his passing, and about their mediumship session.

From Nick's family:

Nick was born on Tuesday, July 22, 1997, six days early, at ten pounds even. Perfect, healthy, and the second of three children, Nick was the only boy between two sisters. Nick lived up to every expectation someone could have for a brother and a child. He loved to play with his sisters and served as a guide, protector, and confidant for each of them.

As a child, Nick was happy and active. Not one memory of him lacked his glowing smile. He had a very witty humor that combined clever and silly in a perfectly amusing manner. He gave everyone nicknames and always knew the best way to lift spirits and lighten moods.

An exceptional athlete, Nick never failed to impress, no matter the sport, no matter the skill. Yet, ever humble and modest, Nick had a gracious personality. He played baseball his entire life and loved the game — he played in college where he majored in communications, with the hopes of becoming a sports broadcaster. You knew when he walked into a room, and it was not just his 6'3" stature. He had a presence about him.

Nick loved music of every kind and never feared testing the limits on the speaker system in the house. He was adventurous, spontaneous, and remarkably generous. We always joked that his heart was bigger than his wallet, as he spared no expense for a friend.

Nick included everyone. No matter what it was, he wanted all his friends and family to be together. He was always planning trips, outings, and family gatherings for us all.

He was a source of light and love. So many of his friends considered him their "best friend," as did each of us in the family. He was easy to talk to, nonjudgmental, and would do anything to help, even for a stranger. It still amazes us the amount of people, some we don't even know, who have reached out to share how much he impacted them. We have been overwhelmed by the love and support we have received since his passing. Nick was so full of life, and he lived life to the fullest, but still he understood the fragility of it all.

Nick was a collector of things and when he liked something he went all in. At two-years-old his first love was trains. He shared this love with his Papa, who worked on trains for a good part of his life. One day while playing with his Thomas the Tank trains on his bed, he discovered that one was missing. We searched high and low and eventually found it between the mattress and bed frame. I decided to use the situation as a teaching moment for my almost then three-year-old son. I explained that it is important to take care of things so they will last, and added that someday when he was grown up, he would want to give his kids his train set and other favorite toys.

He looked at me very seriously with his big, brown eyes and said, 'No Mommy. I'm not going to grow up.'

I laughed and said, 'Yes you will.'

He then said, while shaking his head, 'No, Mommy. I'm not going to grow up. I won't be a daddy.'

This was very alarming to me. During my pregnancy I had unexplained anxiety around him. I didn't experience this with my girls, so I attributed it to him being a boy. Although I never brought this up with him again, throughout his life Nick would make comments implying that he wouldn't live past his twenties. When I would reply with, 'Don't say that.' He would again give me that same look with those big, brown eyes.

Shortly after his third birthday we were traveling to upstate New York to visit family and all three kids became ill with a stomach virus. They all improved after a couple of days, but Nick started saying his neck hurt. When we returned home to New Jersey I took him to the doctor, concerned about possible meningitis. The doctor diagnosed it as "wry neck," and suggested physical therapy. After weeks of no improvement and the stiffness becoming worse, we pushed for an MRI. The diagnosis was an extremely rare bacterial bone infection which called for round-the-clock intravenous antibiotics. They had to put a peripherally inserted central catheter picc line (PICC) in his arm and we had to administer his medications at home for nine weeks. He recovered from this, and although we never knew the cause, we tried to move on. Little did we know that this would be the beginning of six total hospitalizations due to rare and unexplained health issues over the course of his twenty-three years.

When Nick was three-and-a-half, we moved back to upstate New York where our family was from. This was the third move for our family, but the first move for Nick and his younger sister, Gabrielle. We would go on to move to Florida, Texas, and finally Pennsylvania. During our five years in New York, my father, 'Papa,' passed away from cancer. Although my children were young — seven, five, and three — they all had a very special bond with my dad.

About two years prior to my dad's passing, I had discovered John Edward, the medium, on TV and I became very interested in the metaphysical. I had shared the idea with my mom, that my father would be able to 'communicate' with us through electricity. My mom then told my father before he passed to communicate with her via electricity after he passed, and he did just that! It was only moments after his passing that it began, and it continued for many years. Having had that experience, I shared with my children what I believed was possible and they witnessed the electrical validations.

My husband and I had grown up Protestant and we were attending church with the kids as frequently as we could when they were young. Our faith would be tested when we moved to the South, first Florida and then Texas. Having moved multiple times, my children had to start over, and living in different places really helped them to be open and accepting of others.

While living in Florida and playing every sport, one day Nick watched the movie, 'Angels In The Outfield.' It was life changing for him. He decided then that baseball would be his only sport, and that Papa was his angel and had his back. At eighteen, he had Papa's name tattooed on his right shoulder. Papa's birthday was October

18th, and his sister Olivia's is March 18th, so Nick wore number 18 on his jersey throughout his collegiate baseball career in their honor. This is now one of the numbers we associate with him, and feel is significant. Another number is 22 because that is his sister, Gabrielle's, birthday. These are the two numbers that Daniel posted when he was searching for Nick's family, feeling that it was his age, although he was actually 23.

In May 2019, Nick graduated from college and began working for a sports cable company as a field reporter. He was very happy to be done with school and excited about the possibilities in the future. He was working as much as he could and was setting up a new role at work when COVID hit and shut down all sports. He was disappointed, but he made the best of it. He was at a meeting at work where they were explaining the shutdown when he started having terrible pains in his stomach. He wound up going to the emergency room and was hospitalized for five days with unexplained pancreatitis. This was his sixth, and final, hospitalization at twenty-two years old. After this, he came home to recover and to figure out his next steps — these six months of quality time was one of the positives of the COVID shutdown. He was always good at seeing the silver linings.

By August, he was starting to feel restless as there was no end in sight to the COVID pause on sports. He took a position as a sales center leader with the same company his dad worked for. With his friendly personality and his communications background, he quickly fit in and made an impact. Also, at this time, he and his girlfriend were becoming more serious, and things were going well as Nick was transitioning into the next phase of his life.

On March 6, 2021, Nick passed tragically in a car accident with his girlfriend and best friend. It was the worst day of our lives. Our world was shattered. The pain and disbelief were unimaginable. We were paralyzed with grief. Each day I would wake up and pray it was only a nightmare but soon it overtook my dreams as well.

After surviving six hospitalizations, overcoming monstrous odds, he was taken in a second. There wasn't a moment of peace — just unbearable sadness. A family friend, who is spiritually connected, reached out offering help. Having had experiences with mediums in the past, I immediately asked for assistance in finding a reputable medium. She gave us some leads and we did have several readings over the course of the year. We received messages that validated that Nick was with us, but these always left us with more questions and wanting more. Before each reading I would pray and ask for validations. Some were answered, some were not. The one-year anniversary of Nick's death came, and we struggled through it.

The reality was finally setting in. The weeks following the anniversary seemed to bring a new level of emptiness and anguish. Randomly I would find myself sobbing uncontrollably and asking him, 'Why?' and telling him that I needed to know that he is happy. After sharing my difficulties with family and even close friends, I discovered that they were also experiencing this same level of suffering.

I woke up Saturday, April 2, 2022, to a text message from my friend, Ellie, the medium. She shared that a medium she follows on Facebook was looking for the family of a young spirit. Upon seeing the message, I knew it was Nick. At least 90% of the details fit without a stretch. One of the first personal details, Franken Berry® cereal, left no room for doubt. It was literally in my kitchen cabinet along with a box of Boo Berry® cereal. Nick loved Halloween and monsters his whole life, so I would buy the cereal in October as a treat. After he passed, we bought them in honor of him. Within two hours of hearing about Daniel's post, we were on the phone talking to Daniel.

Our minds were totally blown. This man, someone we never met, or even heard of, reached out to find our family to help bring us some peace. It was Saturday morning, and he was with his three kids taking them out for some family time. While driving, Daniel shared who he was and why he practices mediumship. He gave us a reading and in doing so gave us a piece of Nick. Daniel brought forth Nick's personality which is full of love and humor. This confirmed to us that it really was Nick. When Daniel explained that this kind of thing has never happened to him before, we could only laugh. Nick can be very persuasive. It was like we were talking to him on the phone. Daniel's gift is truly amazing, and his selflessness and compassion are tremendous.

I know that Nick chose Daniel for a reason — that being Daniel's love of God, family, and unwavering faith. Nick found a way to communicate his love for us, our need to believe, and to let us know that he is 'okay.' As Daniel shared Nick's messages, it brought a profound sense of peace and healing.

There is no question that Daniel was communicating with Nick. Daniel was able to portray Nick's free spirit, down to his singing and constant joking. There were specific messages for my husband and daughter, messages that were much needed and right on point. It was clear that Nick is present with us every day, as Daniel validated upcoming events, places, and people we would be seeing. The most important message we received from Nick is that love never dies and that we will be together again. We just need to keep the faith.

Our family is so grateful for Daniel's persistence in finding us, sharing his gift, and bringing healing to our family. There is no greater loss than the loss of a child. Daniel's compassion and grace enable him to be the perfect channel between parent and child, bearing the heavy weight of grief while teaching our family how to find a new path for love to flow.

–Amy

CONCLUSION

You are so much more than you think you are. In the simplest of terms, you are energy, you are eternal, and you are Love. Those words don't really do much justice to who you truly are. When you "die," you don't really die, you just change form. Your consciousness simply returns to spirit energy. When you realize this, you can understand that our loved ones who have passed before us, are still available to us. They are not "dead." Their human bodies have exited your reality, but their energy, their love, is with you forever.

I know I didn't say this much already, but you don't need to visit with someone who says they are a "medium" for you to be able to connect and share love with your loved ones who are not in a physical body anymore. You can connect to spirit anytime and anywhere. All you need to do is pray, trust, and pay attention. Your loved ones who have passed, can, and will communicate with you when it is supposed to happen.

You can increase your ability to communicate with spirit by raising your energetic vibration. As a review, we accomplish that by loving, having compassion for others, smiling, listening to music, doing things you enjoy, sharing, being positive, eating healthy, meditating, praying, and trusting in "God," or "The Universe." If you have not read my first book, "Why Are We Here? Reflections On Life From a Spiritual Medium," please do. It will teach you how to raise your vibration and enjoy life on your highest path.

We are all made of energy, and as Einstein proved, energy cannot be created or destroyed. It simply changes form. So, you, my friend, are eternal. Your body, or who you think you are, will die. But you, the real you, lives forever. Your passed loved ones are just in a different reality and I can confidently say they all will be "waiting for you" when you get "there."

From what I can tell, you only get this one life in the body you are currently in. When the real you (your eternal soul), leaves your physical body – the vehicle your soul chose to have these experiences in – you are done with *this* life experience and your reality moves to another one of God's many mansions.

While you are here, I want you to enjoy your life regardless of what the Universe has placed in your reality. Please make decisions that best align with your soul (love). Do the right thing. Choose love, compassion, and forgiveness every day. And enjoy life responsibly! YOU GOT THIS! Much Love!

–Daniel

ABOUT THE AUTHOR

 Daniel is a father, husband, son, spiritual medium, and faithful servant of God. He has been a practicing medium and spiritual teacher since 2018. His mission is to teach and spread God's unconditional eternal love for all. Having completed over 2,500 mediumship sessions, while reading hundreds of books about life and the afterlife, and with many years of Bible study, Daniel has become a "medium" between our true Home (Spirit), and the world we live in. Daniel feels we are all God's children and that every single one of us we will experience eternity in bliss as spirit with "God" when it is our time to do so.

OTHER BOOKS BY DANIEL JOHN

Available on Amazon.com

LINKS AND RESOURCES

 Daniel John's official website:
www.danieljohnmedium.com

 Daniel John's official Facebook page:
www.facebook.com/danieljohnmedium

 Daniel John's official YouTube channel
www.youtube.com/danieljohnmedium

 Daniel John's official Instagram account
www.instagram.com/danieljohnmedium

 Daniel John's official TikTok account
www.tiktok.com/danieljohnmedium

 Daniel John's official mediumship certificate:

www.findacertifiedmedium.com/mediums/ny/geneva/daniel-john/

Made in the USA
Middletown, DE
20 November 2025

21070413R00095